Reinbach

Reinhart

Kanan

Miyabi

Lady Eliaria introduced her friends to her family.

By the Grace of the Gods

Roy
Illustrations by Ririnra

BY THE GRACE OF THE GODS VOLUME 9
by Roy

Translated by Adam Seacord
Edited by Nathan Redmond
Layout by Jennifer Elgabrowny
English Front Cover & Lettering by Jordan Voon
English Print Cover by Kelsey Denton

Copyright © 2020 Roy
Illustrations by Ririnra

First published in Japan in 2020
Publication rights for this English edition arranged through Hobby Japan, Tokyo.

Find more books like this one at www.j-novel.club!

Managing Director: Samuel Pinansky
Light Novel Line Manager: Chi Tran
Managing Editor: Jan Mitsuko Cash
Managing Translator: Kristi Fernandez
QA Manager: Hannah N. Carter
Marketing Manager: Stephanie Hii
Project Manager: Kristine Johnson

ISBN: 978-1-7183-5388-6
Printed in Korea
First Printing: June 2022
10 9 8 7 6 5 4 3 2 1

Contents

Contents

⟿ Chapter 6 Episode 18 ⟾
Lord of Fatoma

After the hunt the following morning, I decided to speed through lunch to prepare for my meeting with Lord Fatoma. As the villagers were already aware of the meeting, they served me lunch before the others, which I appreciated... But after a certain point, I could no longer taste my food. The other members of the Pier, seated at the table with me, seemed to share my sentiment. After all... Lord Fatoma had joined us at lunch.

"Mmm, delicious!"

The lord was a pig beastkin, as I was told; a species overweight across the board. With his kimono and bun on the top of his head, I couldn't see him as a noble or lord, but as a sumo wrestler. Much becoming of his stature, he was currently chowing down on an entire bowl of rice with at least four sides.

To recap how I found myself in this situation...

Lord Fatoma had sailed across the lake to the village and arrived early due to the wind or something. The village chief, not about to keep the lord waiting, tried to fetch us, but Lord Fatoma countered that *he* was the one who was early, and wanted to wait, to which the chief insisted that the lord at least have lunch while he waited.

And so we were sharing our lunch table with a noble lord whom I had never met before. As it would not have been prudent for someone of his status to wander about alone, he was flanked by attendants, even as he ate. One of them was young and resembled a samurai, with scales covering his right eye. The other was dressed like a sumo wrestler, the same as his lord, with scales on the bottom of his palms and wrists. Both of them appeared to be dragonewts, which checked out, given what I'd heard about Lord Fatoma inviting dragonewt scientists from their land.

"Another bowl, please." The sumo wrestler-looking attendant ate just as much as the lord... Maybe he wasn't a bodyguard after all. Seeing how the samurai didn't touch his food and kept a silent watch on his surroundings, I wondered if he was the sole guard for the lord at the table.

In any case, I had to finish my own lunch.

■ ■ ■

After lunch, Lord Fatoma said with a contented sigh, "My, that *was* a feast. The women here sure know how to cook, many thanks. Chief, I truly appreciate such a warm welcome, even while you are surely preparing for winter. I didn't exactly hold back my appetite. I'll have food delivered to you presently; it's not much, but I hope it will add to your winter stock."

"An honor, my lord," the village chief replied.

Lord Fatoma had not betrayed his reputation as a down-to-earth and kind ruler so far. At the very least, it looked like he was going to repay his hosts, and he didn't seem like the type to be boastful about his title or expect unquestioned hospitality for it.

"So, you are the adventurers in charge of protecting this village," Lord Fatoma acknowledged. "Allow me to formally introduce myself. I am the lord of this territory, Count Porco Fatoma. First and foremost, I thank you for your aid in the village's defense."

"Thank you, my lord," Shin spoke for Sikum's Pier, visibly nervous.

Lord Fatoma saw this and gave a smile. "No need to be so formal. Let us be frank with each other."

With that, I could see the weight being lifted off of their shoulders.

"All monsters, not merely mad salamanders, have been on the increase these past few years," he continued. "Which is why I had reached outside of the territory to recruit adventurers... But this year, the numbers are through the roof. Monsters have raided whole stockpiles from a few villages where we just couldn't muster enough to mount a solid defense."

I didn't know things were so dire in other villages.

"I know this village was threatened by just as many salamanders, but it's been a huge help that you have not only defended the village perfectly, but allowed us to allocate manpower to other villages."

"We can't take credit for that, my lord..." The Sikum's Pier collectively turned to me.

"I've heard that a young tamer contributed greatly to the improvement in the village's defense, but surely that doesn't discount the dedication of others involved. I thank you all for your contribution. And for your honesty!" The lord laughed, lightening the mood.

"And... That tamer would be you, right?"

"Correct. Name's Ryoma Takebayashi."

"My pleasure. The village chief tells me you have a letter for me."

"Yes, from the duke of Jamil, R—"

"Reinhart?!" Lord Fatoma shouted in surprise.

That surprised me. Was something wrong? "Yes. I have it saved in my item box. May I retrieve it?"

"Yes, I would very much like to see it. Cast any magic you need."

I produced the letter with the count's permission, and he personally took it from me. From what I had heard before, people of high status like him usually had one of their guards take anything from an unfamiliar source in case of an attack. Lord Fatoma, however, seemed unconcerned by that... He opened the letter and intently read the whole thing.

"Hmm… Ryoma, was it?"

"Yes."

"Did Reinhart say anything when he gave this to you?"

I recalled when he had given me the letter. "Only to seek you out if I was in any trouble because he trusts you. Come to think of it, it did seem like he was holding something back."

"Holding something back. I see… Ha ha ha ha!" Lord Fatoma guffawed, culminating in a pig-like snort. Everyone at the table, the lord's attendants included, looked just as confused as I was.

"Beg pardon," the lord said after his laughter finally calmed down. "Reinhart thinks very highly of you."

After catching his breath, he continued. "The letter describes you as very talented, so much so that Duke Jamil is considering hiring you as a technician. It also has a request to help you with whatever is troubling enough for you to come to me. He even asks that I refrain from recruiting you since he found you first."

"Really…"

"It's rare enough that Reinhart writes a letter to anyone, but I didn't expect to read anything like this. What a treat," he remarked, his expression incredibly kind. I watched him for a few seconds when he looked up and caught my gaze. "Ah, I see he hasn't told you much. Are you wondering why I, a count, speak of Reinhart, a duke, without using his title?"

"No, I wasn't…wondering about that, but now I'm curious about your history."

"Another honest one. In short, we were schoolmates."

"I see. So you've known each other for quite some time, then."

"We do keep up appearances in public, of course, but we're close enough to speak frankly in private. Which is to say, I have a few embarrassing stories about him under my belt. Most likely, he didn't

13

give you any details because he didn't want to speak too much of his school days; there are certainly times when he tries to play the part of a ruffian."

"Really…?"

"I would know. Only natural, considering his environment… and being the son of the renowned Duke 'Dragonflame' Reinbach. If you haven't heard of Dragonflame's claim to fame—"

"He signed a contract with a divine beast," I chimed in.

"That's right. His school years were hindered by having such an accomplished father, garnering him both great expectation and harsh comparison. As a noble, he couldn't afford to show any flaws, no matter how small."

"I never realized…"

"That meant close friends were hard to come by. I just happened to share the same burden of living up to my father… Though I dare say, I had it much easier than he did. Maybe that's why we naturally got along and sought advice from each other. All good memories, now… Oh. Look at me prattling on; I'll never get to the point if I keep this up."

"Thank you for such an interesting story."

"We'll discuss it again some other time. But now I'm sure."

What was he sure about?

"A tamer who uses many slimes and has a good relationship with Reinhart… Your name is known to me, Ryoma, but if I may ask… Do you not run a laundry shop in Gimul?"

"Yes, I do."

"I knew it! You're the Barley Tea Sage!" Lord Fatoma exclaimed, leaning over the table.

I, on the other hand, was thoroughly confused.

"The Barley Tea Sage…?"

"I trust you know of the traveling Semroid Troupe?"

"I do! We crossed paths this past summer."

"Then there is no doubt about it."

Apparently, Lord Fatoma had heard a tale of a traveling bard who sang of a 'sage' who saved a poor farming village by teaching the method of making a new drink called barley tea. As it turned out, the bard was staying in a nearby town at the time, allowing the lord to invite him and hear the song for himself. Moreover, the bard confirmed that, while parts of the song were embellished, there really was a village that was saved by the introduction of barley tea.

He wanted to speak to me after hearing this and discovered that Reinhart knew of the Barley Tea Sage. Just as Lord Fatoma was planning to ask Reinhart to introduce him to me, he caught wind that someone matching the Barley Tea Sage's description—i.e., me— was already in his land. And so he decided to pay us a visit at short notice, as a sort of thanks for our contribution in the hunt.

I hadn't expected the Semroid troupe to come near these parts, and certainly not for Prenance the bard to actually write a song about barley tea. And then for Lord Fatoma to hear of the rumors and decide to come see me—it's a small world, indeed.

I was glad that the troupe seemed to be doing well. What did the lord want to seek me out for, anyway?

"Two things," Lord Fatoma explained. "But no need to place too much importance on them. Nothing urgent, really, so I will take no offense if you refuse. Firstly, I would like to create a dish that this land can be known for."

"A local delicacy, like barley tea?"

"Indeed. Roads being paved during my father's rule had led to an influx in the population and the economy of the land. I'd like something other than fish that would bring people in.

Of course, I only ask for a dish because I want to taste it," he said, patting his portly gut. "I've sent word to towns throughout the land. Despite many suggestions and recipes, none of them have struck me as sensational. I would appreciate any hints or ideas from an outsider's perspective. The second favor I would like to ask of you relates to your talent as a launderer; there is a mountain across the lake from here, near the summit of which stands a hot spring that my father was very fond of, and a cottage he had built near it. I would like to hire you to clean them both."

"Is there something preventing an ordinary cleaning crew from doing the job?"

"After my father passed, I neglected the place, being caught up in adjusting to the job. Grime piled high and solidified, and now there are spots that I cannot clean at all, no matter how many times I send a crew out there... Do you think you could do it?"

"Grime can come in all shapes and sizes, so I can't say until I see the place in person..." I recalled that I had the morning off from hunting the next day. "May I go visit the cottage tomorrow? If it looks feasible to do so, I'll clean it while I'm there."

"You'll take a look?! I'll have a guide ready tomorrow morning. If you can clean it, there's ten small gold coins in it for you."

Ten small gold coins was an exceptional sum for a job like this, and the table began muttering as much.

"Is that not too generous, my lord?"

"I think it to be perfectly adequate. Not only is it a tough cleaning job, but I consider the cottage a keepsake of my father's." Lord Fatoma's tone was casual, but his eyes were slightly downturned.

"Understood. I'll do it for your asking price."

Lord Fatoma beamed and thanked me before leaving the dining hall.

16

Once all was said and done, it was a rather easy encounter, considering how nervous I was in the beginning. Not too bad for our first meeting, especially given the help of Reinhart's letter.

As I watched the lord's boat depart from the shore among a crowd of villagers, I regretted not asking why he was dressed like a sumo wrestler...

⚏ Chapter 6 Episode 19 ⚏
Hot Spring Cleaning, Part 1

Early next morning, I was atop a small boat crossing the lake with the guide Lord Fatoma had sent and the members of Sikum's Pier, who had volunteered to help me.

"I didn't know you could sail a boat, Kai."

"In our village, everyone can. Right, guys?"

"It's got to be our biggest mode of transport."

"You could be going to a big city for supplies or taking someone sick to the next village, but going by boat is the quickest way. Kids learn to sail a boat from their parents, whether they're fishermen or not."

"I see." *Different landscapes call for different modes of transportation, I suppose.*

"Look at that, Ryoma," Thane said.

I followed his gaze. "Those are...isle rats, aren't they?"

Kei had told me about them during the tour on my first day here. They were lake-dwelling monsters that resembled an otter or beaver. I could see a group of about seven or eight of them pushing their raft-like nest.

"Once you see them moving their nests, it won't be long until there aren't any more mad salamanders. And that's the end of the fishing season."

"Really?"

"Apparently, they can sense the waves of salamanders swimming up the river. At the end of the season, they move their nests from the lake to the mouth of an outflowing river and spend the winter there."

"If they move them sooner, the salamanders might destroy their nests."

Peyron and Shin's interjections were helpful. The isle rats watched the monsters in the water to gauge the flow of the seasons. The sign of shifting seasons meant that mad salamander hunting would soon come to an end, and with that, my days in this village.

I resolved to enjoy every day I had left in this little fishing village and to leave no adventure neglected.

■　■　■

The boat carried on across the lake for another thirty minutes as we chatted away, and we reached the port of a large town.

While the setup on the shore looked similar to the village of Sikum, this town had far more docks and a much larger processing station. Even in the wee small hours, there was a constant flow of boats going in and out; many of them were likely shoppers from other villages. The large population on the shore was creating considerable hustle and bustle, and I could see large buildings along the streets beyond the beach.

"Hey!" A man called repeatedly to us from a dock, waving a small flag in one hand, apparently directing traffic.

Kai steered the boat as directed, and we tied it to one of the vacant docks.

"All right, we're good to disembark now."

"Thank you."

"Brr, I'm freezing."

"It's pretty cold out on the lake at this hour."

"Let's grab some hot soup," Peyron suggested. After that ride through the chilly, nearly wintery air, nobody objected to that idea.

It seemed like a lot of other people had the same idea, as the main street off of the beach was lined on both sides with food stands selling hot soup and stew. Just from a short glance, I counted sixty stands. I would have had a hard time deciding where to eat, but the Sikum's Pier crew kept walking.

"Do you have a place in mind?" I asked.

"Huh? Oh, right. We haven't told you, Ryoma, but our brother has a food stand here. We pretty much always eat there when we come."

"I see."

We soon arrived at the food stand, where the team quickly said their hellos and ordered before jumping into catching up with each other, introducing me to the people there in the process. While there was some difference in ingredients and seasoning, the dish did remind me of their mother's cooking.

With our stomachs full of warmth, we headed directly towards Lord Fatoma's manor.

In about twenty minutes, we arrived via the communal carriage. The lord's manor stood at the end of the main street, a straight shot from the beach. It was an ordinary mansion, as contradictory as that seemed, unlike the duke's manor that resembled a castle. It was functional, but rather plain. Despite the large size, it didn't seem as impressive but reminded me of an apartment complex, given it was built from brick. Fencing encircled the building, and a pig beastkin stood guard at the gate.

We told the guard our business, and he responded very promptly. "We've been expecting you. I'll call down your guide straight away."

Soon, the guide came out. "Thank you for your patience, Ryoma Takebayashi. And you all must be the Sikum's Pier. My name is Pigu; I'll be serving as your guide today."

"Nice to meet you," we answered.

Pigu appeared to be in his fifties, sixties, or perhaps older, but I couldn't tell for sure. He was another pig beastkin on the portly side, his saggy cheeks contributing to a kind, grandfatherly look. He had prepared us one of the count's carriages for the day, so we climbed right in.

We reached the mountain with the hot spring within the hour, but then...

"Whoa!"

"Thane!"

"I'm okay! Just slipped!"

"Careful now."

"With how steep this path is, you'll roll all the way down."

"Terribly sorry..." Pigu panted. "There were...more accessible... paths back in the day..."

"Shin. Everyone. Can we take a break?"

"Yes, I think that'll be best."

There were stairs on the first part of the path leading up the mountain to the hot spring, but that quickly turned into a steep hiking trail that we had been struggling up for the last three hours.

Eventually, however, we did reach the hot spring.

"Is *this* the hot spring?" I asked.

"A bit different from what I pictured," Kei said.

I could smell the sulfur, hear the water, and see the steam ahead, but the only building I could see was a dingy shack.

"Yes, it is... *Pheoink*... The last lord who built it disliked decorations. He said that it only needed a small cottage..."

"Could I take a look inside? You could have a seat while we inspect the place, Pigu."

"Absolutely. Here's the key. There isn't too much room in there, and I'll be right here if you need anything."

The road was apparently a bit too rough for someone his age. He sat down on a bush, or rather, an old bench covered in vines.

We opened the cottage door with the key. It really was a tight space, barely fitting the lot of us—five adults and a child. Considering the girth of Lord Fatoma, this cottage would have barely been large enough for him, let alone any company. The only things in the tiny cottage were a few chairs, some clothes baskets, and a hand-drawn map on the wall, but they were covered in dust and cobwebs.

"Cleaning here shouldn't be a problem, so there must be something else..."

Straight across from the entrance, we opened another door and found a narrow set of stairs that descended three steps into an open, outdoor bathing area.

"Oof..."

"This is something..." Shin muttered.

"It's seen better days, that's for sure," Peyron chimed in.

The bath simply drew water from the hot spring into a large tub. From a cursory glance, I could see that the hot water flowed over the tub, across the floor and through the drainage trough to dump the water outside. However, the drain seemed to have been clogged by the leaves and branches that had blown in. The draining had stopped, and something other than sulfur was stinking up the area. And that wasn't all.

"I wonder if there's iron in the calcium carbonate." The tub, and even a large area of the floor around it, was covered in a thick layer of buildup. Reddish-brown chunks speckled the mirrors on the wall alongside handprints of the same color. These solidified minerals wouldn't be easy to clean.

"Let's start with what we *can* do. *Dimension Home*." I called out the scavenger slimes and had them drink up the puddles of water, leaves and all. "Be thorough with that clogged drain, please."

Sensing the scavengers' compliance, I stepped outside.

Pigu called out to me nervously. "Is something the matter?"

"I'm draining the water from the bath, so I'm preparing for our next course of action in the meantime."

"I see… Do you think it can be cleaned?"

"Well… I assume the buildup is what's giving you trouble?"

"It is indeed. I've tried cleaning it myself, but I've never been able to get it off."

No surprise there. The minerals in the water had been deposited by the change in temperature or pressure. In Japan, this kind of spring sediment was said to give hot spring locations a sort of character. On the other hand, they also posed a problem for those maintaining the spring, since it caused buildup on the tub, floor, or drain, as I witnessed here.

Pigu had gestured a scrubbing motion, complete with a bitter, defeated expression, but I doubted that scrubbing alone stood a chance.

"This is a bit of a spur-of-the-moment idea, but I'm going to create a fluid that could get rid of it."

"You can make such a thing?!"

"Hopefully it'll work." With earth magic, I crafted a pot that would hold the cleaner. Then I summoned some sticky slimes and acid slimes and had them spew sticky solution and acid. "That buildup is called calcium carbide. It's a similar material to seashells, and susceptible to acid, so I think this should do the trick."

"Really?!"

"In theory, anyway."

I expected the acid would melt the buildup like an acidic cleaner would, but I didn't want the acid to be too powerful and end up damaging the floor or walls, so I diluted the acid with the sticky solution in the hope of raising its viscosity as well.

I experimented with the mixture for a while until it looked good.

"Right, time to try this out," I said, and returned to the bath.

Since the scavengers had already drained the tub, I decided to test out the cleaner on a corner of the tub. I had the acid slimes form a small circle and carefully poured the cleaner into the center.

"Wow!" Cheers erupted behind me as the Sikum's Pier watched the cleaner rapidly bubble from the acid, reacting with the calcium carbide. While the acid was activated just fine, it still seemed too concentrated for cleaning, and it was more viscous than pure acid, but not by much. I decided the mixture needed a little more work.

After several rounds of experimentation, I created three different variations of the cleaner—a more acidic and less viscous one for thick layers of buildup, a less acidic and more viscous one for thinner layers of buildup and for the walls, where the cleaner would drip more easily, and a third variation with an even balance of acid and viscosity.

≈ Chapter 6 Episode 20 ≈
Hot Spring Cleaning, Part 2

Two hours later, the Sikum's Pier and I had finished administering the acidic cleaner all over the outdoor bath and decided to take an early lunch in front of the cottage.

Our lunch, spread across a picnic blanket on the ground, consisted of the usual soup and rice balls prepared by Kai and Kei's mother. The rice balls were packed with stewed fish, its powerful *umami* pairing perfectly with the rice.

As I was enjoying my lunch and the fair weather, I heard a voice coming from the mountain path we had climbed that morning.

I was wondering who would come this far up the mountain, when Lord Fatoma parted through some trees, followed by the two dragonewt guards. "Bfft! A rough trek as always... My!"

"Lord Fatoma?!"

"Sire?!"

"You showed them yourself, Pigu?"

"Of course. No one knows the way here better than I."

"That much is true. And I did tell you to pick anyone you want. But think of your age... Oh, well. Seems I'm intruding on another meal."

"No, Lord Fatoma. You're not intruding... But what are you doing up here?"

"Hm. I simply couldn't get this cleaning situation off my mind. I had to take care of some urgent business, but I came as quickly as I could. Do you think you can clean it?"

I showed him the tub and gave him the rundown.

"I see… There's a substance that can melt that rock-like grime."

"I had to make do with what I had today, but it works."

"Sire, I've witnessed the experiment myself. He says the cleaner is soaked into fabric, which is sitting on the grime to let the cleaner sink in, but the surface of the buildup was already starting to melt."

"After an hour or so, I'll take the fabric off and begin the cleaning process."

"How exciting," Lord Fatoma happily walked out of the cottage.

We stepped outside to find the Sikum's Pier and spotted the two guards, who looked rather uncomfortable with each other's presence and weren't talking to each other.

Lord Fatoma apparently noticed too. "I haven't introduced them, have I? This is my guard and assistant, Sir Kichomaru. And the master of sumo, the traditional martial arts in the land of dragonewt…"

"Tairyuzan's the name. An honor to make your acquaintance."

"He is a certified *yokozuna*, the highest rank achievable for pursuers of sumo. In addition to guarding me, I have him coaching me in sumo."

After the two bowed upon finishing their introductions, we moved on to introducing ourselves. I went last, after the members of the Pier. It all seemed to make sense now.

"So you *are* into sumo, Lord Fatoma."

"Hm. I thought you were looking at me differently. You know of sumo, Ryoma?"

"I do. My grandparents were adventurers when they were younger, and they've told me stories. I didn't expect to meet a real *rikishi* here, though."

27

"I discovered sumo in my student years. One of my classmates was a dragonewt. Once he told me about the sport, I knew it in my heart. Pig beastkin will easily gain weight and keep it on, giving all of us a signature *plumpness*. But I hear that hopeful *rikishi* overeat on purpose to achieve this body type. What's more, if we tried to train in the sword, for example, the first step would be to lose weight. Combined with our weight, overworking can often injure our knees, but sumo teaches training methods that are conducive to this body type. We pig beastkins were practically born for this martial art." Lord Fatoma had always wanted to learn sumo since those days, and when he invited scientists and began importing crops, he also invited the *yokozuna* Tairyuzan. "Speaking of, Ryoma, can I ask you something?"

"Absolutely."

"The bath was covered in fabric. I understand its purpose, but do adventurers always carry that much fabric around with them?"

"Well, most people wouldn't, but I can use space magic, so it's not a problem for me. Besides, I can use that fabric as bandages or to make my clothes, so I bought them in bulk at a discount."

"Is that garment your own creation?" He pointed at my faux-down jacket in surprise, so I confirmed. "Interesting… On our return boat yesterday, we were discussing how warm your outfit looks. Apparently, there's something similar in the dragonewts' home."

I turned to the pair of dragonewts. "Were you talking about the *hanten*? A short throw-over—"

"That's right!"

"You know what a *hanten* is too? You know a lot about our homeland."

"Thank you. I heard most of it from my grandparents, but I also have an acquaintance from there."

"Fascinating."

"Hm. He is the Barley Tea Sage, after all," Lord Fatoma brought this up again.

"That title's a bit too much for me."

"Why not? You are very knowledgeable."

"But Sire, when many hear the word 'sage,' they think of *the* Lady Meria. Perhaps a comparison between such a legendary figure is not one Sir Ryoma welcomes."

"Hm. You may have a point there. I apologize."

"Please, there's no need."

"And you said the cleaning will take a while longer?"

"Yes. I want to let the cleaner soak in some more."

"Then I'll come by later to check on the progress. I'm really looking forward to seeing your work."

"Thank you," I said.

Lord Fatoma and his guards left us, passing through the trees again. "Are they going to climb all the way down the mountain and walk back up?"

"No, I believe Sire has gone to visit the grave of his father. It was built on the top of this mountain, in accordance with his final wishes. Sire laments that he can't come over often, so the cleaning job might have been the perfect excuse."

"That's good to hear." The previous lord's only indulgence was this hot spring, and he was also buried here? "He must have really liked this mountain."

"Yes... Whenever he had the time, he would walk up this mountain. He even built this bath himself."

"Wait... He did it himself? I thought he hired a builder."

Pigu gently smiled, reminiscing. "He wasn't the kind of person to spend money on himself. Whenever he could, he worked to make this path."

29

"I've heard a little bit about that; it was a very arduous process."

"Yes. He wasn't the only one to consider building a path here. However, all of his predecessors were unable to build through the swamplands and overgrowth. But he spent his own money and got his own hands dirty... After tireless efforts, he finally paved a path up the mountain. On top of maintaining the manor, he even cleaned this spring himself every time he made the trek. He was frugal, through and through."

I couldn't argue with that, all things considered... I glanced towards the cottage and spotted the map on the wall through the open door.

"Is everything all right?"

"Well, I was looking at the hand-drawn map."

"What about it?"

"It looks like a map of this land, but something's strange about it."

Why was there a map here, anyway? It was the only thing about the otherwise strictly functional cottage that seemed to stick out like a sore thumb. Not to mention that the map was framed.

"That is a hot springs map."

"Hot springs?"

"Yes. This is not widely known, but there are mud pockets throughout Fatoma. If you look at the paths on the map, they are concentrated around those pockets. Some of the paths do not exist, so he must have drawn the map before making detailed plans. I imagine that he wanted to market Fatoma as a hot spring sightseeing destination once the paths were completed."

"I see." As I didn't know anything about the mud pockets, I doubted it had to do with this odd feeling I felt from the map. I took a good look at the map again... To no avail.

"Isn't it about time, Ryoma?"

"Yes. Let's get back to cleaning."

I wrapped some fabric around my face for a mask and wore cleaner slimes instead of gloves. After taking off the fabric soaked with the acidic cleaner, I used a pressure washing spell to wash away the cleaner. The water pressure helped peel off the crumbled buildup. This didn't perfectly clean the surfaces, but that much was expected.

From this point, I asked the Sikum's Pier to help me, providing them with what protective gear we could fashion, and having them re-apply the cleaner or scrape off what buildup was left.

"Hey! It's a lot easier to get it off now."

"Same with the tub."

"Looks like it seeped in through these thin cracks."

"It's definitely weaker. I think we can smash them."

They chiseled away large chunks, and I had my slimes work on some tough spots as needed.

After another two hours, we were completely done!

∼ Chapter 6 Episode 21 ∼
An Odd Feeling and a Chance Revelation

When Lord Fatoma returned, I asked him to give the place a once-over.

"Incredible! I can't believe it all cleaned up this well."

"Looks just like it used to…" Pigu chimed in.

They seemed very happy with the fruits of our labor.

"Thank you, Ryoma," Lord Fatoma reiterated.

"I'm glad it's to your liking." That being said, I was curious about a section of the hot spring that he had told me not to clean. "Are you sure you want the faucet untouched?"

The end of the waterline was still mostly in the same state as it was before we started cleaning, even though it had some buildup blocking some of the water flow.

"If I asked you to clean that, I doubt you'd finish it by day's end. The line goes all the way down to the source of the hot spring. Besides… I really do appreciate your thorough cleaning of the place, but I rarely come up here to use the cottage myself. I only wanted to restore it to the fullest possible extent to have as a memory of my father. I think that what you've already done is more than enough. If anything else, I would have hoped to see the view from here again, but the bamboo's simply grown too much…"

"We definitely neglected those too," Pigu added.

"So the bamboo wasn't always here?" I asked.

"No. Back in the day, my father planted a bamboo shoot he had brought home from somewhere a little ways away from here.

He often brought me fresh shoots to eat. And now, after years of neglect, this is how it's ended up."

"We used to have a wonderful view from here…"

But now, the bamboo largely obscured any and all scenery from the entrance of the hot springs. The members of Sikum's Pier looked to me, then to the entrance, and then to the changing area. They were clearly up to the task, so…

"Then, let's finish up by cutting down the bamboo by the bath to restore that view," I proposed.

"You'd do that? I mean, I don't wish to put pressure on you," Lord Fatoma clarified. "But are you sure about this?"

"Of course. I'd be happy to do it for ten small gold coins, or even for free. Plus, those five seem up to the task themselves."

"Wha—"

"Hey!"

The Pier was obviously startled as we turned to them. *They didn't have to sneak around like that. Plus, considering that reaction…* As if to prove my point, the lord approached them, making them completely tense up with bashfulness. I decided to prepare for the task in the meantime.

I produced a wire slime and a stick from the Dimension Home, and a sturdy wire to help me safely climb down.

"A little heads-up would've been nice, Ryoma!"

"Not everybody's got the social skills to handle nobles like you do…"

Kei and Kai put their arms around my shoulder.

"Lord Fatoma seems pretty down to earth. Just act natural and you should be fine."

"You're pretty ballsy for a kid…"

"And here I thought we were at fault for being hicks. Clearly, he's the problem."

I resent that. You think I don't get butterflies in my stomach having to deal with people above me? Especially when I've never met them before?

I decided to put the matter aside and move on to business—not that we were doing anything too technical. "The slime and I will chop down most of it. Speed over accuracy and all. We'll probably miss some spots here and there, so I would like you all to cut those. It's quite steep over there, so use this safety rope, please."

That was all it took. They already trusted my slimes thanks to the work we'd done so far. The team quickly got ready as I headed over to the edge of the outdoor bath. I climbed over the middle of the fence line I set up for safety and lowered myself down.

"I'm counting on you."

The wire slime quickly and enthusiastically stretched its body into a long jigsaw blade. It could stretch as much as forty meters, but I asked it to make two strands in either direction, each a bit shorter than twenty meters. Once I saw that it was stretched out long enough along the ground, I had it connect both ends to form a large hoop. Then, the core of the slime stretched out a sliver of itself to hold onto my stick, through which I sent in energy to enhance the blade.

"Try to stay as close and flat to the ground as you can. Let's do this!"

The wire slime began tightening the hoop until the blade dug into the bamboo trees, then it started moving the blade left and right as it contracted the hoop some more. The enhanced blade was sharp, allowing it to quickly chop down the bamboo on the exterior and contract towards the next batch.

All in all, it barely even took ten seconds to chop down all the bamboo and vegetation within the area I specified.

"I thought about this during the experiments after its evolution, but it's rather like a chainsaw. It's kind of scary what they can do... Oh?" A shadow was cast on the ground, and I looked up to find Lord Fatoma's surprised expression.

"Have you ever seen a slime do that?" he asked the team.

"Uh, I think Ryoma's slimes are special."

"Just the other day, he felled a bunch of trees around the village as an 'experiment.'"

"Yeah, the old folks of the village said they wanted one of those slimes. It'd save them a lot of time gathering firewood."

The wire slime did have impressive cutting power. Heck, I was using a stick to make sure I wouldn't accidentally touch the blade.

"I'm going to keep chopping them down like this," I called up to the five, who had entered a kind of spectator mode. "Go ahead and come down after a couple of cycles!"

I turned around and chopped down a twenty-meter patch of bamboo, before lowering myself down another meter and chopping down twenty meters in either direction. I repeated the process, creating a forty-meter clearing down the slope.

The copious amounts of bamboo kept falling towards the bottom of the mountain, much of it being held up by the still-standing bamboo trees and their leaves. Soon, it seemed to be approaching critical mass; I needed to be careful and not let them crush me as they fell.

I remembered how a lot of fictional characters fought using wires or strings and wondered if I could do the same with the wire slime. Not that the current method seemed conducive to combat, but the slime was able to cut through bamboo quite easily.

I could get used to this method of transportation...

I was thinking of a zipline, and how it took some time to climb down the abandoned mines. Maybe I would try to set one up, at least one way. On the thought of more applications for the wire slime, I returned to contemplating fictional "string users." Not that it mattered, but I felt like all string-wielding characters were pretty powerful, whether friend or foe. In fact, I couldn't recall a single string user who couldn't fight. With the abundance of protagonists who stuck to commentary in battle-oriented series, I would have expected one to come to mind...

"Whoops." After briefly being lost in useless thoughts, a view opened up below me. I was nearing the precipice of woods composed of non-bamboo trees. With how open my view was, I expected that they could see much farther from the bath above, so it seemed I had chopped enough bamboo, but I had a strange feeling about the view, which I kept my eye on as I climbed back up to the bath.

When I reached the top, I realized why.

"Oh."

It had to do with the direction I was facing. Outdoor baths were traditionally built to overlook the best view possible, and the bath above had been made with an open view over this slope. Subconsciously, I had expected to overlook the beautiful Lake Latoin once the bamboo was cleared. But the bath overlooked the direction opposite the lake, over an area of swamp and trees. My compass had been put off through the winding hike, and I must have nearly realized that when I saw that map. Not that I had paid much mind to direction during the hike, since we had Pigu as our guide, and I could have sent my limour birds to scout for the town if he had gotten lost—*note to self, room for improvement there*—but I was still curious as to why the bath opened in this direction. Not that the view was bad, but it was a familiar one in this land. Perhaps it had to do with the location of the hot spring source.

I returned to the bath, and to Lord Fatoma's approval of the bamboo clearing. I asked where the source was, and he told me that it was actually closer to the side of the mountain that overlooked the lake, and his father had drawn the water all the way here. That meant there was a good reason for building the bath this way.

I couldn't get the thought out of my head, so I asked the Sikum's Pier crew to pack up a few things that were left and went to think on the matter as I took in the view.

"The materials...and the construction..."

A possibility entered my mind about what kind of person the previous lord was. I made some guesses based on my hunch and reached a hypothesis.

"Pigu, sir," I called.

"Yes?"

"You told me earlier that the grave of the previous lord is at the summit, right?"

"I did. Is something the matter?"

I asked him a question to test my hypothesis, and it seemed like it was a hit.

Pigu looked astounded. "How did you know? There is almost nothing surrounding the grave. We felt bad about leaving the ground so bare... But we had been left detailed instructions in his will, on everything from the location of the burial ground to how to maintain the trees."

"Thank you, sir. I think I've found a way of meeting the lord's other request."

"I'm glad I could be of help," Pigu said, looking like he still wanted to ask questions.

But I was more worried about putting my newfound clue into action.

⇐ Chapter 6 Episode 22 ⇒
Experimenting with Slimes
and Ryoma's Deduction

That night, we had returned home, our labor having been rewarded with high praise and the promised ten small gold coins from Lord Fatoma, which were split evenly between myself and the Sikum's Pier. Well, at least that was my intention, but they insisted I keep it since the knowledge, cleaner, and slimes used for the cleaning all came from me. Only when I insisted that I would feel horrible leaving them without any pay after they helped me with the job did they agree to my terms.

After splitting up the reward, each member of the Pier hurried off to buy their own desired amenities—drink, food, or some sort of household item—before taking the boat back to the village. This had led to us having to rent another small boat to get all of us and the merchandise back to the village. Even when we returned to the village, people spotted their haul and started a commotion about how we'd hit the jackpot. It was a lot to deal with, but I had fun.

I stretched my legs out in bed, reminiscing about the day.

"Well, I got the cleaning job done, and I have a clue regarding the new dish... And best of all, I found a new use for the acid slimes. All in all, a pretty productive day... Oh, right. One last thing before I turn in..."

I produced the leftover acidic cleaner from my Dimension Home in its container, along with the conches I had been feeding the pearl slime. When the acid slime first evolved into a pearl, I'd thought of the resemblance to mayonnaise pearls, but I had another thought come to mind after today's cleaning job. To test the hypothesis out, I made sure the pearl slime saw the conches as food before soaking one in each of the three acidic cleaners. Soon, bubbles began to form on the surface of the conch in the most acidic variation.

Once the frothing stopped, I rinsed the conch with water and had a cleaner slime wick all the moisture and other impurities away. The shell had begun to dissolve, but there was still some sand attached to it. I repeated the process three times until I was running low on cleaner, so I decided to let it soak overnight. After returning the slimes and my tools to the Dimension Home, it was time to hit the hay.

■ ■ ■

The next morning, perhaps out of curiosity about the progress of my experiment, I woke up earlier than usual. After making preparations to leave, I checked on the conches I had soaked overnight.

"Just as I expected."

The cleaner had dissolved the outer layer of the conch, revealing patches of pure white. I gently buffed those patches, and a beautiful nacre was revealed. Nacre, just like pearls, was a lustrous substance composed of calcium carbide from the shell. In addition to the type of shellfish that create pearls, some conches also contain nacres. One of those species famous in Japan was the marbled turban, the meat of which was edible. Although the marbled turban was a saltwater shell...

"*Appraisal*."

Sandril

A freshwater conch that uses its mucus to adhere minute sand and pebbles to its shell for camouflage. Edible, and most often consumed steamed. However, the heat of cooking it will cause its nacre to lose its luster.

"The lake had a similar shell, and it evolved into a pearl slime by eating the hidden nacre... That makes a lot more sense than trying to connect acid + egg = mayonnaise to mayonnaise pearls." I'd finally gotten a satisfying explanation for its evolution.

"Now, what to do with this information..."

Serelipta—who was *technically* a god—had told me that pearls were even more valuable than I thought. I expected to be able to turn a shell with the same glimmer into a quite popular product... We'd passed a jeweler's stand on our way out of the city yesterday, but out of all the jewelry made from vibrant shells, I didn't see any using shell nacres. Considering how I was able to acquire so many of these conches as trash from the villagers every day, it was safe to say that they only saw them as food.

It seemed like an incredible waste. Still, I couldn't give any of this info to the villagers, let alone Nikki. Just like Serelipta said, that would be extremely dangerous. Even though I had connections with Lord Fatoma, I was hesitant to tell him as well. I didn't take him for a bad person; we'd barely spent two afternoons together, but after a few conversations with him over dinner, it was plain to see that he was indeed down-to-earth and deserving of the respect his people gave him. I doubted any of it was just an act, but all the same, something was bothering me.

"I wonder if Lord Fatoma is lacking in strength... Or maybe he's further down on the noble food chain."

There was one particular thing which brought that thought to mind—the goblins we had encountered when we were searching for Nikki. I'd heard that other nobles would occasionally send goblins to Fatoma as a form of sabotage or harassment. There was no proof to back up those rumors, but I had seen the goblins with my own eyes, and we did come across a cage, which implied some sort of human involvement with the goblins' appearance. And this was apparently a common occurrence.

Something wasn't right. Even though those goblins were relatively weak, they were still monsters. Someone could have gotten hurt, or worse. Nikki would have been in serious danger if it wasn't for his secret lair. So why was nobody doing anything about this recurring problem?

It would have made some sense if Lord Fatoma didn't care about his people, but that went against their perception of him, not to mention mine. Maybe it wasn't that the problem was being ignored, but rather that it *couldn't* be addressed. I did hear something about how Fatoma's wide-open layout made it difficult for the lord to deal with sporadic harassment like that, and that the land was so poor that the people were starving until the travel road was eventually built.

Protection against monsters and enemies required soldiers, and soldiers required food for sustenance. Eagerness wouldn't fill an empty stomach, after all. How could a land whose people were already starving afford to maintain an army? Even if some minimal level of force had to be kept to defend the land, there still wasn't enough food for everyone. Without enough food to go around, one way to minimize the suffering of the people was to keep the army's numbers at a minimum.

So one possible explanation for this was that Fatoma simply didn't have enough fighting power. If that was the only problem, though, Lord Fatoma could just ask neighboring lords for help. That would come with a cost, of course, and perhaps he just found the idea too shameful. But was it that much more shameful than the level of incompetence being displayed by refusing to deal with the goblins' harassment at all? This led me to believe that Lord Fatoma did not have a good relationship with his neighbors. While I didn't take the rumor about how a noble from the neighboring land was responsible for sending the goblins at face value, it certainly checked out. And people were talking; if all this was true, logically, they would have figured it out by now.

The thought reminded me of something I witnessed in my days as a student. Early in my middle school years, I came across a typical bullying scene; the same thing that happened at every school. I helped the male student that was getting beaten up, and asked what happened. The student told me that his bully had gone to the same grade school as him, so he decided he wasn't going to tolerate any more bullying from him once they both entered middle school. He'd started learning karate a month earlier. He'd boasted about that to his bully, and the bully proceeded to beat him up even worse than usual.

The kid was too honest for his own good, really. I understood how he was sick of being bullied, and he had every right to object to it. But what did he expect to accomplish by telling his bully as much to his face? There was no guarantee that a teacher could solve the problem, but there was no point in trying to fight back on his own without training well enough first. Furthermore, it would have only been prudent to keep it a secret until he was ready to fight. He was just a cocky amateur who gloated a little too much.

He'd done nothing but show his own hand, and that caused the bully to ramp up his aggression.

Why would an oppressor wait for the oppressee to grow stronger when they'd declared their intention to fight back? Of course there would be retaliation if they openly declared as much.

"Maybe Lord Fatoma is the same."

He had invited scientists to Fatoma to improve food production and also learned sumo. Both of these seemed to be implying a desire to improve his own situation. Perhaps he was trying to build his strength under the guise of not being able to deal with the harassment? If that was the case, any information about pearls or similar valuables was extremely hot property. As Serelipta's warning reminded me all too well, it would only bring danger to those too weak to protect it.

"I'd better not tell him any of this... But it doesn't change the fact that these things exist in the water. Someone will have to catch on eventually."

Serelipta had said it was a jewel that could not be harvested in Rifall yet. He was the kind of god who blurted out whatever thought happened to occupy his head at that time, and I didn't see a reason for him to lie about this. The key word here was "yet."

"Oh?"

I heard footsteps. The morning was fast approaching, and I decided to put my thought process on hold. I still had a few more busy days ahead of me, after all.

⁓ Chapter 6 Episode 23 ⁓
The Village Festival
and a Local Delicacy in the Making

Three evenings following the hot springs cleaning gig, I found myself in the village plaza with most of the village's population, who were crowded around bonfires, cauldrons, and tables upon tables of food.

The isle rats had built their nests to shut off the river flowing out of the lake, which led to the number of mad salamanders drastically decreasing within that timeframe. The fishermen in the area and villages at large, Sikum included, had been notified of the fishing season's end by the fishermen's union.

Preparations for a festival celebrating the end of the season had been underway since this morning, using the last catch of the year and food brought in from the city. In fact, the festival was just about to begin. There was just one thing left...

"The lord has arrived!" A male villager announced as he ran into the plaza.

Led by the village elder, a line of village higher-ups formed a line to greet Lord Fatoma. I quietly filed in at the end, and we headed to the beach.

Just as we reached the beach, Lord Fatoma came ashore.

"Thank you for coming, my lord."

"My, thank you for such a warm welcome." After greeting the village elder, Lord Fatoma approached me. "And thank you for the invitation, Ryoma. I've been looking forward to this."

"Likewise. I know it's asking a lot, but really, thanks for coming out here."

Upon finishing cleaning the hot spring, I realized that Lord Fatoma had never specified when and how he wanted me to propose the potential local delicacy he had asked for; perhaps this was down to him being more concerned with the cleaning job. I asked him to come to Sikum's end-of-season festival, where I would serve him the dish. While I wasn't sure how he would take it, he gladly accepted my invite.

And so, here we were. On this day, Lord Fatoma was accompanied by his two dragonewt guards, Pigu, and another pig beastkin, whom I was told was the head chef at the count's estate, while we made our way back to the plaza.

Once we got there, the proceedings formally commenced. Apparently, these things didn't have a set schedule; they just started once the villagers decided that everyone was ready. The village elder and Lord Fatoma each said a few words, but they kept things succinct.

After that, we headed to a corner of the plaza, close to the statue that I had once prayed to. Beside it, I set up my specially made magical cookware.

The head chef immediately showed interest in it. "This is a very large and highly functional cookware, especially for being portable. And you even have a hot plate, a large oven, and enough space for four pots... Splendid!"

"I know a talented craftsman, so I had it made to order. Camping is a big part of adventuring, but I try to eat a hot meal whenever I can. Luckily, I can use space magic, so it's not an issue if my equipment's on the larger side."

Lord Fatoma gave a chortle. "You're quite the foodie, I see. I've met my fair share of adventurers, but I've never seen anyone with your array of equipment. And looking at the crest on the cookware... Perchance, did this come from the Dinome workshop?"

So he knows about them. "Indeed it is. Very perceptive."

"Perception is nothing if not a curse all nobles must bear. One wouldn't want to be the odd one out at a party, so keeping up with all the latest trends is a necessity," he chuckled with an air of self-deprecation. *I guess even nobles have it rough, in their own way.*

"The dishes I'm going to present to you today are best served hot, so I'll be cooking them now. Preparation is already taken care of, so it won't take very long. There are plenty of other dishes for the festival as well, if you would like to enjoy those in the meantime."

"How exciting. What's on your menu?"

"If you want my recommendation, I suggest the oden. Some of the villagers have tasted it themselves, and I've been told by them that it's a more elaborate version of their usual soup. It contains fish, tofu, and vegetables. Having it with ground horice made it more closely resemble the local soup dish, and it was popular among my tasters. Fortunately, I was able to receive assistance from someone who makes great tofu, so I'm serving fried tofu, a meatless burger, some inari sushi—"

"Sushi? Did you say sushi?" One of the normally expressionless dragonewts was now evidently giving me his full attention. *I think they said his name was Kichomaru, or something...*

"Oh, yes, I did. Inari sushi, to be exact. The kind wrapped in fried tofu." *Is he a sushi guy?*

Lord Fatoma interjected. "Kichomaru has a strict diet as a part of his training regimen."

"I see." *Figures.*

Just as I was wondering whether I should have asked about the guards' dietary restrictions, Lord Fatoma added, "But there are exceptions to everything. One of them *was* sushi, I believe."

"That is correct. My exceptions are sushi, tempura, and sukiyaki."

Well, that's…strangely specific. Getting odd feelings about that… Sort of a "the only Japanese foods foreigners knew about a decade or two ago" vibe… Then I remembered what Asagi had told me when I was still new to the Gimul area. The dragonewt settlement was created out of the actions of a past traveler, who was evidently a foreigner with a decidedly *skewed* perspective of Japan.

"Well, I'm glad that there's something on the menu fit for your consumption. I have everything I need to make sukiyaki and tempura as well. It may be a little different from what you're used to, but would you care to partake?"

"Really?! I would love some of that…'inari' sushi, as you called it, and some sukiyaki and tempura as well."

"Coming right up. I also have zong, dirty rice, kinpira-gobo, and fried or spiced lotus root."

"We'll take one of everything," Lord Fatoma ordered.

"You got it. Now, then…"

I asked the village elder to gather the simpler orders while I began preparing my ingredients: mixing into soup, steaming, grilling, frying…

"Hm. You're frying shredded fish or crushed tofu and occasionally re-shaping them by mixing vegetables. With this much variety, I wouldn't soon become tired of this."

"This fried tofu has a gentle flavor too. The dashi's seeped into the breading and everything."

"I love lotus root enough already, but when it's fried like this…"

"I thought it was some strange take on the sushi since I don't see it at home, but the inari is quite enjoyable."

"Remember how our homeland had dirty rice and kinpira? My, this brings back memories..."

As high praise came my way, I remembered to finish up with a dipping sauce.

"Thank you for your patience. Now, this is what I most highly recommend—gyoza."

The table was occupied by plentiful dishes that were now nearly cleared, so I exchanged some of the empty plates for plates of freshly prepared gyoza.

"Hm. It seems you've wrapped something with a flour-based dough and grilled it. I saw the same thing in soup, fried, or steamed... But they seem identical at their core."

"That's correct. I have employees from Gilmar, who've told me that they have a similar dish there."

"A Gilmar dish, eh? Let's give it a try."

"I've prepared eight variations of dipping sauces. Please dig in."

Lord Fatoma and his attendants each plopped a gyoza into their mouths.

"Mm! Hot, but delicious!"

"Indeed. One bite of the grilled gyoza, and the meat just about melts in your mouth."

"It makes for a wonderful combination with the soup."

"Great texture as well on the fried ones."

The group continued to compare the variety of gyoza, which were well received...except by Lord Fatoma, who looked a bit disappointed. I wasn't surprised, seeing how I only prepared ordinary gyoza.

"It *is* delicious. But..."

"It won't be a local selling point, will it?"

"Mm. The gyoza is made up of pork and vegetables wrapped in flour. Rice flour, for the steamed gyoza... Unfortunately, almost none of the ingredients are sourced locally. We have a decent importation infrastructure right now, but we can't push this as a local dish if it's made entirely of imported ingredients. You, of all people, should know that. You're telling us to make a gyoza with different ingredients." Lord Fatoma took the words right out of my mouth.

"Indeed. I only intended to make suggestions for today, and I prepared these gyoza as a sampler of this simple yet versatile dish."

"Versatile?"

"First of all, as you said, gyoza uses a flour-based wrap to enclose other ingredients; it was pork and vegetables today, but you can have various other ingredients, and as many of them as you like. The wrap can be made from any powdered grain as well. For example, I've used rice flour for the steamed and soup gyoza. That was just my preference, but I wanted to show that there are at least two options when it comes to wraps. There are four different ways to cook them— boiling, grilling, steaming, and frying. I was already able to prepare eight different sauces. Even ignoring the infinite combination of ingredients inside the gyoza, that's sixty-four combinations in all. You can also enjoy them neat without any sauce, and combined with a variety of ingredients..."

"Hrm... Very intriguing. The variety is practically limitless."

"That was my thinking. So, I had some of the villagers prepare some gyoza of their own."

"What?"

I gave the village elder a glance, and he swiftly came right up to us.

"My lord, members of our villages have these gyoza ready. It would be a privilege if you could taste them..."

"How kind of them. I would love to."

A line quickly formed, each villager bringing their own gyoza concoction. First was an elderly woman, bowing to Lord Fatoma as her grandchild supported her.

Lord Fatoma ate the gyoza. "Hm... A gyoza in horice soup. Very soft and warm."

"Thank you, my lord. My husband and I are too old for harder foods now... I thought it best to use familiar flavors."

The second in line was a burly fisherman, who was clearly intimidated. "I-I almost never do anything in the kitchen, but I hope you appreciate it..."

"Ha ha ha. It's not as shapely as some, but this grilled gyoza is quite tasty."

"Th-Thank you, my lord! My wife's expecting, so I wanted to make something energizing!"

Third came a portly woman, who seemed more confident in her cooking than the rest.

"Delicious!" Lord Fatoma explained. "Juicy swamp shrimp with julienne-cut lotus root... Wonderful texture."

After the fourth and fifth tastings, Lord Fatoma began to look concerned. "Well... They were all delicious, and I cannot argue with this dish's versatility. That makes choosing one all the more difficult."

"I don't think you need to choose just one," I suggested.

"How so?"

"What if you had the people of each village and region in Fatoma concoct their own gyoza? Some of them may receive the blessing of the lake while others may not, for example. While fish is fresh and plentiful in Sikum, other meats are rarer. Perhaps there are regions closer to the border of Fatoma where meats, vegetables, and flour are easier to come by."

"Hm, indeed there are. You make a good point about the difference in their culinary culture. Come to think of it, some of them might serve me the same meat-based gyoza you first served me... I see. If I were to give each locale autonomy to create their own gyoza, people across Fatoma could enjoy a variety of flavors. If that appeals to merchants and nobles passing through Fatoma, that could energize those regions."

There were cities in Japan that famously gained their renown through gyoza, such Utsunomiya and Hamamatsu, and you'd be hard-pressed to come across someone who didn't like them. Setting this up as a sort of friendly competition within Fatoma had the potential to further encourage each region to thrive. Another thing on my mind was the unoccupied buildings dotted along the travel roads of Fatoma that were opened as shelters for travelers; I asked the lord about them.

"Those were lodgings for the workers, used when my father was having the road paved. They've served their purpose, but it would only cost money to demolish them. It rains quite often here, so I decided to open their doors to help out travelers... What about them?"

Staffing them would be a hurdle, but it seemed like a waste to leave those buildings abandoned. *What if they could be made into the equivalent of rest stops on Earth?*

Lord Fatoma considered my suggestion. "Hm... If we want to spread the word about Fatoma's gyoza, we need as many people as possible to try them firsthand. Even those not looking to stop here for long will still need to eat... Even if they eat on their carriages, fresh gyoza will be more satisfying than a bag of dried meat. Soup could be a hard sell, but I can see travelers buying grilled, fried, and steamed gyoza. Perhaps there could be a workaround for the soup as well. As it happens, I've been thinking about those buildings a fair amount myself. To prevent bandits and other types squatting in them, I've been sending patrols out to inspect both the buildings and the road. I could have them stationed..."

Once I explained to him the ideas of rest stops and drive-thru restaurants, he was surprisingly receptive to the idea. Hearing him pondering over stationing guards brought to my mind the neighborhood police stations in Japan.

"Even if there are only one or two guards in there at any time, travelers will feel much safer if there are stations along the road they can visit in case of an emergency."

"I concur. Plus, gyoza doesn't seem too complicated a dish to prepare. One of the villagers who offered me some earlier mentioned he isn't normally the type to cook. If gyoza is that simple to learn how to make, it should be relatively easy to spread it to other villages."

"Yes. I think that many of the natural foods in Fatoma get a bad rep on appearance alone."

Crab and octopus came to mind. They also had creatures similar to squid and sea cucumbers. Octopi were called "devil fish" in some regions, and many cultures flat-out refused to even consider eating them. Such was the gulf between individual food cultures... On the other hand, I could sympathize with not eating things that didn't *look* appetizing.

"If people avoid eating certain foods because of how they look, perhaps serving them as gyoza fillings would help to combat the stigma."

"Gyoza ingredients are ground and wrapped up, after all. Make them bite-size and no one would see what's inside... Ha, ha ha ha ha!" Lord Fatoma broke into laughter that culminated into another porcine snort. This garnered the attention of the villagers, but he continued talking, unbothered.

"Very interesting, indeed. I can tell you've put a lot of thought into this. Many chefs and home cooks have sent me their recipes, but you're the first one to consider how to market the dish. Of course, I've only advertised for a recipe. When I asked you to consider this, I didn't expect you to give me such a well-thought-out solution, especially for someone your age. This may be embarrassing for you, but I dare say that you live up to your reputation as the Barley Tea Sage. Or the Barley Tea and Gyoza Sage, perhaps?"

It seemed I was rapidly becoming a summertime staple. As practical as ever, Lord Fatoma continued. "There are issues on my end with logistics and whatnot, so I can't make a decision tonight, but your proposal deserves serious consideration; your idea has a great deal of merit to it. Thank you."

"You are too kind. I was only able to make this suggestion because we went to the hot springs the other day. Otherwise, I would have served you a hot pot with local fish and tofu."

"Oh? I would certainly love to try that as well sometime... Still, I remember our prior conversation. Would you mind sharing your thoughts?"

The biggest factor was that handwritten map; it was the only non-necessity in that cottage. Anyone who's tried it knows that drawing a map is harder than it looks. Of course, drawing a little map of a neighborhood was one thing, but drawing an entire territory, including the main roads and topography, on the other hand... Only someone who knew the land like the back of their hand could do that. I never could have done it myself, at least. Even if the previous Lord Fatoma knew the land well as part of his job, I figured there might have been some reason or significance in hanging the map in such a private retreat.

Something I only discovered because of the details in the map was that the mountain with the hot spring was one of the few mountains in the territory, and the tallest one at that. So, the summit of that mountain was the best spot to oversee most of Fatoma. Considering how he had his grave built there, I could only imagine how much the previous lord treasured Fatoma and its people. Looking at the map, I had only traveled a small portion of the roads in the territory, which made sense, since I'd gone directly to Sikum for mad salamander hunting. I hadn't even made so much as a detour on the way. I only knew about other hot springs in the territory because Pigu mentioned them to me while we were looking at the map. I'd had a wonderful time in Sikum, but it seemed like Fatoma had so much more to offer that I didn't know about yet.

"I started looking at this request in a different way." I didn't know enough about this land to come up with a local delicacy, so I only had to ask people with that knowledge to cook the dish. Considering the point of creating a local dish in the first place... "I eventually thought of gyoza. But I was so caught up in my thoughts that I caused quite a stir within the village."

"How so?"

"I was thinking about this at the hot spring, and I spoke to you before we left."

"When you invited me to the festival, you didn't...?"

"All I could do was ask the villagers for forgiveness."

I, an outsider, had decided without their permission to invite their lord! There was no way they could uninvite him either. I still felt kinda bad about it. I even asked the villagers to make their own gyoza so I could present them to Lord Fatoma. I felt so bad about manipulating everything the way I did that I ended up trying to help out around the village as much as I could, which seemed to surprise the villagers.

54

"You have a one-track mind."

"True. I'm just lucky the villagers were so accepting." My eyes drifted over to the village elder, to whom I gave a bow.

"We were surprised at first," the elder explained, "but having our lord at the festival is a terrific honor. Besides, all of us owe the previous lord a great deal, especially old codgers like myself, so we were glad to be of assistance. You even donated expensive beef for the festival and set up some sort of magical barrier to keep the plaza warm. No one took offense to any of it, so I say we should just enjoy the festivities together. My lord and company, there are still plenty of dishes to be had. Please, enjoy the festival to your hearts' content."

I really couldn't thank them enough...

"Well, it's nice to see everything worked out," Lord Fatoma said. "By the way, there's a boy who's been watching us for quite some time now. I think he wants to talk to you, Ryoma."

"What?"

I turned in the direction the lord was pointing to find Nikki, who was now flustered by the numerous sets of eyes directed at him. I quickly waved him over to dispel the tension. "This is a friend of mine. He's proven to be of great help with all the preparations as well."

"Is that so?" Lord Fatoma turned to Nikki. "What is your name?"

"Nikki, my lord!"

"Well, Nikki, thank you for all of your wonderful help. Thanks to you, I've tasted many delicious dishes."

"R-Really?" Nikki chuckled, looking nervous for once, but happy. "We've got a lot more good grub where that came from! Right, Slime Guy?"

"What?" That took me completely off guard.

"More, you say?"

What's he on about? I've already served all of the dishes we prepared...

"That thing, remember?" Nikki insisted. "You were doing all those 'experiment' things with that new, evolved slime!"

"You mean the ash smoking one?"

One of my slimes, which had eaten ash, had newly evolved sometime during the past three days; I'd found it in my charcoal oven a while back. It just fed on ash day after day without doing anything much of note, until it helped itself to the ash discarded from the hearths throughout the village and evolved into an ash slime, as one would expect. Incidentally, its stats were as follows.

Ash Slime
Skills: Disperse 3, Condense 3, Absorb Moisture 5, Dry Out 5, Disinfect 3, Consume 1, Absorb 2, Split 2

The ash slime was the driest slime I had ever encountered, resembling a powdery pile of ash. That explained the Disperse, Condense, Dry Out, and Disinfect skills. It kicked up ash every time it moved and whenever there was a breeze, but the particles returned to the pile on their own. Additionally, it didn't drink water like other slimes. Well, it did drink *some* water, but it seemed to need drastically less hydration than my other species, so it was content with the moisture from the air and the ground alone. In fact, it apparently couldn't handle large amounts of water at all. It could use its Dry Out skill to deal with excessive moisture, though, so it wouldn't have a problem unless someone kept dowsing the thing with water, or threw it into a lake or something. In fact, I was wondering if its Absorb Moisture skill could come in handy like a dehumidifier.

In addition to that, I had come up with ash smoking as a use for it. At some point during my time on Earth, one of my coworkers had gotten me fish which had been smoked under volcanic ash. But my ash slime had been consuming ashes from wood, not from a volcano, and I had only made some fish the same way as an experiment; I couldn't make any certain claims about the taste. Alas, Lord Fatoma was already staring at me with blatant curiosity.

"Now, I'll warn you, I can't guarantee it'll be any good—"

"What? You said they tasted great. Not just the ash-smoked fish, but the eel, sea ruffe, and puffer fish too."

What the hell?! How does he—

"I saw you sneaking out the non-parasitic fish from the haul we got from the processing plant. Figured you were using it to feed the slimes. Weren't you doing that today?"

"You saw me?!"

Those were three fish that were not eaten around here on account of being poisonous. I had secretly been testing a hypothesis, wondering whether I could fillet them properly through Appraisal and the help of a poison slime, and whether I could safely consume it afterwards. And here I thought no one had been watching me.

"Heh! If you think you can slip away from the eyes of Sikum's best prankster, you've got another thing coming, Slime Guy!"

"You little... Oh, never mind."

Eventually, I explained everything to Lord Fatoma. "Are you still interested?"

"Of course. If a fish discarded for its poison could be cooked safely, we will have more food to go around. It would surely make life easier for my people. I wish to seriously consider every insight you have to offer, and if possible, I would love to taste them."

"Likewise..." the village elder muttered.

Back in the city, I had procured plenty of the ingredients and seasonings necessary, including Japanese ones like miso and soy sauce to appease the dragonewts. At this point, I had no reason to refuse.

"Very well. I'll use Appraisal to make sure there is no poison whatsoever."

"Mm. I understand that these dishes are experimental, but I'd be glad to taste whatever you have."

I procured the necessary ingredients from my Dimension Home and took the head chef up on his offer to help me prepare a smorgasbord of ash-smoked barramundi, tempura rockfish, grilled and marinated eel, puffer fish sashimi, puffer fish soup, and puffer fish fin sake.

After the tasting…

"I was curious how it would taste after cooking in ash, but… May I have another?"

"This is delicious!"

"Hmm… Crunchy on the outside, yet fluffy on the inside. Simply exquisite. It would be a waste to turn up my nose at this. I would love another rockfish, some vegetable tempura, and something else."

"Amazing! There's no bones or smell to any of it! What sorcery is this…"

"Pigu, the glazed one is even better. The elegance of the soup and the aroma of the sake pair perfectly with it. To think we have ignored such delectable food out of fear of being poisoned…"

The properly processed eel, rockfish, and puffer fish were well received too. But there was one problem. "I'm out of the ash-smoked fish! Tempura platter's up! Um, I leave the eel in clean water for at least three days before cooking, so all the mud seeps out. And it had a lot of bones, so I did a process called Bonesplitter when filleting it…"

"Save the explaining for later, Ryoma! Next dish, please!"

"Right. Oh, but one more thing! puffer fish may be delicious, but you always have to be careful with the poison!"

"I will keep it in mind," Lord Fatoma answered. I had to concentrate fully on the cooking for now, and I had good reason to…

"Hey, can we taste that ash-smoked thing?"

"One puffer fish sashimi, please!"

"Send some tempura my way!"

"Any more eel over there?!"

Many of the villagers had crowded the area, drawn in by the smell, especially from the marinated eel. With Lord Fatoma's permission to forgo formalities, my portable magic kitchen had become no less bustling than a downtown food stand at rush hour.

"Ha ha ha! This is great!"

"These little buggers always chew up our nets! But from next year on, *we'll* be the ones chewing *them* up!"

"More booze over here!"

"Bring over whatever you got!"

I'm running out of ingredients…!

"We're out of puffer fish! The last rockfish is going in now!"

"How about the eel?!"

I still had some for now, but it seemed it wouldn't last very long…! Just as I considered chopping them into rice, I realized I had some meat gyoza left over, so I fried up my excess rice to pair with it. *I bought some preserved shapaya earlier… If I let it soak in the deodorizing solution for a while, I could sauté it with sesame oil to make a side! For drinks, I could serve some wine I had from fermenting fruit in the drunk slime's alcohol… Heck, I could even try making some cocktails!*

"Hey, we got some extra food over there. You want it?!"

"Yes, thank you!"

May to the rescue with extra food! I still have time to dance!

I was feeling weirdly hyper and elated, maybe because of the electric air of the festival, but it was a lot of fun cooking and serving as much food as I could as the evening darkness grew nearer...

⇜ Chapter 6 Episode 24 ⇝
A Wish and Warning after the Festival

Tuckered-out children and pie-eyed adults gradually trickled out of the plaza until we officially closed the festival late into the night. After that, the village elder and I accompanied Lord Fatoma and his men to the beach to see them off.

"You've seen us far enough," Lord Fatoma graciously said. "Such a wonderful night. Thank you."

"We were all happy to see you, my lord."

"Wonderful," he smiled and faltered for a moment. "Oops... I may have gotten carried away with my drink tonight... Ryoma."

"Yes?"

"I'd like to sober up some before getting on the boat. Would you care to converse with me for a while?"

"Of course."

"Thank you," the lord said, and turned to the village elder.

"I must beg your pardon, my lord. The cold night air is not very kind to my old bones."

"My apologies. I shouldn't be too long, Pigu. Could you take the men to prepare the boat?"

"Yes, my lord."

The village elder began making his way back to the village, and Lord Fatoma's company left us to prepare the boat for departure, leaving just him and me alone on the beach.

Amidst the sounds of the breeze and waves, Lord Fatoma took a deep breath. "Such a lovely breeze. Oh, are you cold, Ryoma? With all the meat on my bones, I find it quite comfortable myself."

"I'm fine. If I get really cold, I can just cast a barrier spell."

"Ah, that's right," he laughed heartily, and rubbed his belly. "As I said, I had a splendid night. Thank you for all the wonderful dishes."

"It was my pleasure."

"This completely slipped my mind, but we haven't discussed your pay for coming up with the dish. Is there any price you had in mind?"

"Now that you mention it…you told me you've searched wide and far throughout the land for a recipe. Isn't there a price already set?"

"I mean a price accounting for the ash-smoking, not to mention your methods for safely cooking three fish we previously thought inedible. Combined with the gyoza idea, they could each generate a new industry in the land; that's certainly worth more than what I was going to pay for a single recipe. Now, the other nobles would scoff at the idea and probably tell me that I can't even discern valuable information when I see it, or worse, accuse me of being unable to properly pay for them. And let's get serious—new projects cost money. I wouldn't mind paying you directly, of course, but I don't think you're the type that prefers money above all else. It'd be better for me if you wanted to negotiate a price of your own."

Fair enough. Reinhart and Pioro had both told me that technology must be treasured… But damn, Lord Fatoma wasn't beating around the bush at all here.

"Let's see, what would I want… For a start, I would like you to ensure that the people are educated with the proper method for preparing those poisonous fish." It was easier to provide them that night because I could rapid-fire Appraisals, supported by my huge well of magical energy, and double-check with the poison slime. "They are still poisonous, after all."

"The villagers should be well aware of that; every parent makes sure their children know of that. I expect the bigger issue will be winning people over to this idea."

That made sense. The excitement of the festival might have helped, but there were a good number of villagers who'd tried at least one of the poisonous fish… The most popular of which was the eel-like one. While the smell of the glaze seemed to help, Nikki had also told me that the eel-like fish was eaten on occasions when they really couldn't catch anything else. Second place went to the rockfish, and the puffer fish-like creature—the most poisonous of the three—was dead last, with most people merely peeking at the dish from a distance, but nothing else. Just as people outside of Fatoma didn't eat octos (that is, octopi) or water spiders (that is, crabs), people here didn't eat eel, rockfish, or puffer fish, least of all the elderly.

"Those in the village who've acquired a taste for it must proceed with caution, but we did warn the elder about that during the festival. Risk is inevitable when it comes to new knowledge or technology—ignorance, carelessness, misuse… But fear of those risks halts progress. You have given us knowledge that may greatly improve the lives of my people. It is my job as the ruler of this land to educate the people on said knowledge and manage the industry, as well as draft rules surrounding it. I will ensure that the safe cooking methods are properly introduced to the people," Lord Fatoma said with all seriousness. He had definitely earned my trust.

"Then please take these." I handed him a pile of documents from my item box.

"Are those instructions on how to prepare the fish?"

"They're records of all my experiments. The fish that I call eel, for example, had sharp teeth and bones similar to another fish I know called the pike conger. A day of soaking the fish wasn't enough, but the odor was mostly gone by the second day. There's also some other data that I've been keeping. I did show the preparation and cooking process to the head chef beforehand, but these documents contain all of the findings I've made through my experiments. I can't guarantee it'll all be useful, but there are things that I haven't even gotten the chance to tell the village elder. I hope this can be of assistance to you somehow."

"Wonderful…! I'd be happy to accept it, but you do realize that this tips the scales even more greatly in my favor, yes?"

"Uh…" *W-Well, maybe I can just call it a bonus with the recipes.*

"In that case… I know! Could I have some of the bamboo that grows near the hot springs cottage?"

Lord Fatoma had said something about bamboo shoots the other day, and bamboo could be used for charcoal on the grill, or for construction. It was a rather useful plant; I'd just need to set up a dedicated space to grow them in my mountain.

Lord Fatoma stared at me for a few seconds before letting out a sigh. "You're too humble… As you've seen, there is an abundance of bamboo growing wild up there, and I haven't done anything with it. You can take as much of it as you like. Anything else?"

At this point, I started considering just asking for money, but that didn't sit right with me. I tried to remember if anything else came to mind. "I heard that Fatoma is famous for its pottery, as well as its fish."

"Indeed, we have a healthy supply of local clay. Would you be interested in some pottery?"

There was an earthen cooking pot that I'd enjoyed using when I was cooking at the festival, so I wanted to buy a few of those. *People mostly use wooden or metal dishware in Gimul, so they might find it fascinating if I brought it back; perhaps I could buy a few extra and take it to Serge's shop. I might even decorate the meeting room of the shop with a good-looking piece of pottery.* Not that I had any knowledge in that sort of fine art, though...

"In that case, I can give you one of the decorated pots from my manor. It's a decently valuable piece, one you could decorate your shop with. I'll also introduce you to my favorite ceramist, where you can pick up any souvenirs or merchandise for your shop. They'll accommodate you to the best of their ability."

"Thank you."

"No need to thank me. This is your payment for completing my requests...not to mention Reinhart's letter."

"If you say so."

Lord Fatoma chuckled. "Speaking of, do you remember when I told you about my relationship with Reinhart?"

"Yes. You were schoolmates, and Duke Reinhart struggled with others' expectations of him, considering who his father was."

"Indeed. My father had built many roads in this land, but Duke Reinbach had accomplished so much more than that, which must have put quite a lot of pressure on him. His family has plenty of enemies as well."

"Right..."

"Of course, considering his family, their power and history, on top of his father's achievements and making a contract with a divine beast, I'm fairly certain no one would be mad enough to start a fight with him head-on while he's alive... Actually, I've started to hear frequent rumors of vandalism in Reinhart's land."

What?!

"He's a smart man," Lord Fatoma continued. "Especially as a student, he was always in the top five of his class, but only because he worked harder than anyone else. He isn't a natural genius... Of course, I'm not saying that he lacks skill or talent. That's not what I want to say..."

He gazed up at the night sky for a few seconds in contemplation before continuing, still staring into the night. "From now on, I am not speaking to you as a noble, and this is not a formal request. Just a personal wish of mine... Would you be so kind as to help Reinhart as much as you can? Talented though he may be, a lord cannot rule alone. He's the type to bottle things up and try to handle everything on his own."

"Really?"

"You seem surprised."

I was, somewhat... I mean, I thought Reinhart was the one who was worried about *me* bottling up my feelings and not asking for help. I told Lord Fatoma as much, and he broke into his now-familiar snorting guffaw.

"A-Apologies, but... I see. *He* told you to ask people for help, did he? I didn't expect him to be unchanged from our school days, but perhaps he's fixed that habit of his. Back in the day, he nearly broke himself because of that. On the other hand, he might have spoken out of his own experience."

He seemed happier now, nodding to his own conclusion. "I'm glad to hear he has people he can rely on, especially if that includes you. After seeing how you've handled my requests, I can see that you have a different perspective on things than the rest of us, and quite expansive knowledge as well. Small wonder that Reinhart wants your talent all to himself. If it wasn't for that letter, I would have recruited you myself."

I was just about to tell him I was honored when he added, "And that's exactly why you must be careful." His jubilant tone had made way for a serious one, as his gaze now met my own.

"I've told you that I intended to offer you those two quests after hearing the rumors of the Barley Tea Sage. The fact that your reputation preceded you to me should show you that your fame, although not many know that Sage to be the adventurer Ryoma based in Gimul, is spreading rather wide. I'm far from the only one who can summon a member of the Semroid troupe, or send someone to gain more intel on you. Reinhart has already warned me as much, and I never intended to ask about everything you've done in the past... But there are people in this world that all too easily cross the line between good and evil once they see money to be gained. Noble or otherwise, not everyone you meet will be like Reinhart and me."

Lord Fatoma had calmly warned me as such, but I felt like he knew more about my past than he let on.

"Thank you for the advice. I'll be careful."

"Mm. You're close enough to Reinhart, so use his power to your full advantage."

Lord Fatoma then performed a long stretch. "Right, I think I'm sober enough now. Don't want to stay out too late," he said, and began packing up. Maybe he had made time specifically to give me that warning, which I really was thankful for.

"Oh, and Ryoma," he added, "when will you return to Gimul?"

I had to pack for the journey home and wanted to buy souvenirs for everyone in Gimul as well as capture some mud slimes, which I had put off in lieu of preparing for the festival, so I was intending to stay for a few more days. That said, I was concerned about the rumors of Reinhart's land becoming more dangerous. I could trust

Carme to run the shop, and I wouldn't worry about security with my staff...but I thought it would be best to expedite my return as much as I feasibly could.

"I plan to get ready tomorrow, and leave the day after at the earliest."

"I see. In that case, I'll reach out to the ceramist first thing in the morning and have them hold onto the pot from my manor for you. The end of the year is a social season for us; we're going to be busy preparing for it."

"Understood. Thank you for doing all of this in such a busy time... and for everything else."

"I had a splendid time. Farewell."

Lord Fatoma told me the name of the ceramics shop before walking onto the dock and onto his boat, which eventually returned to the other side of the lake.

⮞ Chapter 6 Episode 25 ⮜
A Hasty Departure

Two days had passed since the festival marking the end of fishing season. I had bought everything I wanted the previous day, so I had moved on to capturing mud slimes. Serelipta had told me that I only had to use mud magic to find one, but I had never used a mud spell before. That being said, I had seen mud magic before and knew that it was a combination of earth and water magic. I was certain that I'd get the hang of it if I tried hard enough.

"Over here, Slime Guy!"

Nikki and I had come to a particularly muddy spot in the forest.

"Okay, let's give this a try."

Mud magic... In simplest terms, mud was a mixture of water and earth. I combined magical powers of both elements and imagined seeping it down into the muddy ground to make waves in the mud, like the water spell Wave.

If I were to give that spell a name, it'd surely have to be...

"Mud Wave!"

Upon casting, ripples formed in the mud, growing into waves. Just as they crashed into the surrounding trees and swallowed their roots...

"Whoa! Here they come, Slime Guy!"

"Wow... There's so many of them."

The waves of mud were disturbed as a bunch of mud balls appeared one after another, just about thirty of them. Nearly crumbling from the excess of moisture, they tried to scramble away from us.

"Right, just as we planned."

"Let's go!"

Mud slimes slithered across the ground like the other slimes, but quite a bit slower. Nikki scooped up one after another, tossing them into the pots I was producing from the item box. With so many of them, a few had sunk back into the mud, but we had caught twenty-seven of them on our first attempt. I cast Appraisal on one of them.

Mud Slime

Skills: Disperse 3, Condense 3, Hold Moisture 5, Consume 1, Absorb 2, Split 2, Synchronize (Mud) 5

"Seriously?"

"Didja learn something new, Slime Guy?"

"Yes. Its skills are similar to an ash slime."

Disperse and Condense were the same, but it had Hold Moisture instead of Dry Out. Most notably, however, I saw Synchronize (Mud). I had never seen a skill name with parentheses in it before, but it must have meant that it could only synchronize with mud.

This made for another new slime in my arsenal. Since I was able to catch nearly thirty of them in one go, I could gather enough to turn into a big or huge slime with a little more digging. I let Nikki know that I wanted to look for some more mud slimes, and he was happy to tag along.

■ ■ ■

71

The two of us spent the next few hours running through the woods. Using mud magic made it ridiculously easy for me to find mud slimes; it was rather like casting a net into a pond packed full of fish. Taking some breaks along the way, and moving from location to location, I managed to capture and contract over six hundred of them without us straining ourselves too much. No matter where I cast mud magic, there were at least four or five of them that sprung out, so I was wondering at this point if most of the mud in the forest was made up of mud slimes.

"Ooh!"

"What's up?"

"Look, over there," Nikki pointed.

"That's the tree near your secret lair, right?"

"Hold on a minute! I'll be right back!"

Nikki ran off into his lair, so I sat on a thick tree root to wait for him. After a couple minutes, Nikki emerged with something cupped in his hands.

"Here, Slime Guy. They're yours."

"What are these?"

They seemed to be rocks, all unevenly shaped and sized.

"Those are soak lights. You find them in the mud, and you wet them in a dark place to make them glow! They're super-rare!"

"Really now…"

Come to think of it, I recalled how Nikki's secret lair was all lit up when I found him in there; he must have been using these.

"You're leaving today, right? You taught me a whole bunch of stuff, so I wanted to give them to you as thanks. I don't need them anymore, after all."

"You don't?"

To be honest, these fantasy gem-like rocks definitely had me intrigued. But how was he going to have light in his lair without them?

"Kids *can* come to these parts of the woods, but it's still far from the village."

"Yeah, and?"

"After what happened before, I talked with mom and dad…and I decided to rebuild it closer to the village, somewhere they can easily come see and not worry about me. So I don't need them anymore."

"I'm proud of you, Nikki."

"Heh! I'm big enough to help out the grown-ups around the village now! My pranking days are through!"

He was talking about helping out at the processing plant as his punishment for running away, but he did seem to enjoy the work. Maybe that was a good learning experience for him… Still, with all the energy he displayed, I wasn't entirely sure he could keep himself from pulling pranks just yet.

"Say, you wanna go build that lair now?" I offered.

"What about the slimes?"

"We've caught at least six hundred of them already. I'd be happy to help out; consider it thanks for these stones. I'm good with using magic for construction, so just tell me what you'd like me to do."

"Can you build it on a tree?"

A treehouse? I could probably manage a simple one, but…

"I'd have to see the site first."

We hurried back towards the village so Nikki could show me the location, which was on the border of the village and forest, at the corner of the lumbering area where I had visited often. Nikki had his eye set on a tree that had grown too thick to mill and was left alone.

"Dad talked to the village elder and the other grown-ups, so I can use this tree and some of the space around it. He said he'd help me build it too."

"All right… The trunk and the branches are thick enough. They should support a good amount of weight." The big decision to make was where on the tree to build the lair. Nikki had told me on our way here that he had envisioned a tree-top cottage.

"Right! Dimension Home." I called the wire slime out.

"Uh, Slime Guy? You're not going to cut the tree with that, are you?"

I reassured him that I wasn't going to use the wire slime to cut any part of the tree, and gave the slime my orders.

The mangrove-like tree branched out often, so I had the slime pull and bend those branches with its wires to make space. And then…

"Grow!" I cast a spell that made plants grow, making the branches slowly grow in size, digging into the wire. By forcing growth while the branches were bent, I was trying to keep the branches in that formation.

"Wow! You're changing the shape of the tree!"

"There's actually an art form called bonsai, where you change the shape of a tree. That's normally done with a potted tree over years and decades, though!"

I tugged on a thin, flexible branch and wrapped it around a neighboring branch, twining them together. Once they were thick enough, it didn't even budge when I dangled from it. *I ought to set up a swing here. After all, it's not a proper treehouse without a swing, is it?*

"I'll help!"

"Okay, Nikki. I'll cast the wire, so help me pull."

We spent an hour bending the branches of the large tree. Most of the branches now stretched out of the trunk horizontally before curving up. They weren't exactly uniform, but it almost looked like a giant table. You could pass boards through the spaces between the branches to build a comfortably sized cottage.

"I think all that's left is to set up the swing, plus a rope ladder so you can get up there."

"What about the cottage?"

"You should ask your dad about that. He said he'd help you, didn't he?"

"Yeah! We're gonna make a wicked lair together, and when you come back here, you'll totally have to see it."

Then, we gathered up enough lumber and built the rope ladder and swing together, and got it all set up.

"Finished!" We exclaimed together.

Granted, it was just a foundation right now, but I still thought it went well, all things considered. It was almost time for me to take my leave anyway.

"You're leaving, Slime Guy?"

"Not before I say my goodbyes to the villagers first." I had told them that I would be leaving by the end of the day, but it would have been rude to leave without saying goodbye.

We quickly cleared up our workspace and returned to Hoy's house, where I had been staying.

"There he is!"

There was a crowd outside the house, the Sikum's Pier among them. Before I could even wonder what was going on, the crowd swallowed me up as everyone began talking to me at once.

"Heard you're leaving today, kid?"

"Y-Yes! Thank you for everything!"

"You were a great help with our fishing, and the festival too!"

"Why don't you rest up here for another few days?"

"Things have finally settled down after fishing season, you know!"

"Um, I…"

I was starting to get overwhelmed when Kai, Kei, and Shin called to the crowd.

"That's enough!"

"I think you're overwhelming the poor lad."

"Everybody give the boy some space!"

That same moment, Thane and Peyron pulled me out of the crowd.

"You okay?"

"Yes, thank you."

"Sorry about that… They just wanted to see you off."

"Most of us have bugger all to do outside of fishing season, after all."

Even as we spoke, the crowd seemed to be growing. Then, May and her mother emerged from the house and handed me a large leaf wrap. Whatever was inside, it smelled delicious.

"Take this with you, Ryoma."

"Maybe I'll use it for dinner tonight."

Hoy stepped out of the door and said, "Take care."

"Everyone, I have to thank you all for your kindness while I've been here! This was a great experience for me!" I said, loud enough for people in the crowd to hear.

"As long as you enjoyed yourself."

"Hey, take this too."

"Want some mad salamander jerky?"

"Come back whenever you want."

"This is from last year, but it should still be good. If it tastes funky, give it to your slimes."

Everyone in the crowd started chatting me up again, some of them giving me souvenirs and food. I struggled to keep up with all of the energy, but the community around me was so bright and warm... I certainly didn't expect a farewell party this big. Of course, I knew they had more time on their hands after the fishing season, but still... Everyone continued talking, and though I felt a little sad to leave them, almost everyone was telling me to come back whenever I wanted... So I decided there was no need to be mopey about it.

"Thank you so much! I'll be back!"

"Take care!"

"You better come back! We'll be right here!"

"Write us sometime!"

My send-off was a fiasco right to the very end. As I repeatedly gave them assurances that I would be back sometime in the future, I bid farewell to this village full of incredible kindness and hospitality.

⪻ **Chapter 6 Episode 26** ⪼
Interlude — Trial of the Gods and Serelipta's True Intentions

Some time after Ryoma's departure from the village of Sikum, nine gods were congregating in the divine realm. Eight of them sat in a circle, while Serelipta, the odd one out, was sat on a stone seat, confined to it by luminous chains.

"Look, I'm not gonna try and take a powder when I'm surrounded here. Just get me out of these chains, would you? Plus, this seat's beyond uncomfortable…"

"Well, suck it up! Do you even understand what you've done?!"

"Okay, so I broke a rule or two. But isn't this overkill? We may be two members short, but it's not like eight of you are going to let me slip away anyway."

"He's got a point," Kiriluel, the goddess of war, remarked.

"Still no excuse to loosen his chains," Fernobelia, the god of magic and scholarship, countered.

"Are Meltrise and Manolaioa here yet?"

"Hm… I did call for them, but it looks like they're not coming."

"Manolaioa can be pretty moody…"

"Not only that, is Meltrise ever *not* asleep?"

"Well, no point in waffling any further. Let's get this over with," Tekun declared.

Gain, the creator, looked from god to god. "It would have been ideal to have everyone present, but we shall begin regardless. We are here, as you are all aware, to deliver a sentence upon Serelipta, who has touched Ryoma's soul. Wilieris and Grimp have caught him, and Serelipta himself has admitted to doing so. Do I have the details straight?"

"Yes."

"Of course."

"That's right! I admit it, I did it!"

"Good. I must remind you all that interfering with a mortal soul is strictly forbidden. Serelipta will face appropriate measures, but there is room for debate regarding the severity of his punishment. Does anyone have any suggestions? Or words to say in Serelipta's defense?"

Kiriluel immediately spoke up. "Well, personally, I think we ought to hear him out first. It's already bizarre enough that Serelipta took the initiative and *willingly* interacted with a mortal. Surely he must have had a reason."

"Well? What do you have to say for yourself?" Gain pushed the conversation in its logical direction.

With all eyes fixed on him, Serelipta rolled his eyes at Kiriluel. "Sheesh, I gotta have a *reason* for everything? You've all met Ryoma before. Call it curiosity on my part. I touched his soul to take a peek into him; there was talk of something being off about it. I'm not the type to get curious about travelers from the other world, but what about Fernobelia, then? Is that really so hard to believe?"

"I shan't deny I do have an interest in him. But do you not believe that you crossed the line when you touched his soul?"

"Well, at first I was just planning on talking to him, reading his mind a bit, y'know? If you want my honest answer, I got the feeling that I misread something. So I can assure you, I *do* feel quite penitent about this whole thing."

"Your countenance suggests the exact opposite...though, what do you mean by 'misread,' exactly?"

"I've told you a million times already, Wilieris. And when I say 'a million,' I do mean *a million*. Like I said, all I was going to do at first was ask him questions and read his mind. Just tried to make it a teeny-tiny bit easier to access his emotions. *However...* There was a resistance I didn't expect, and he actually negated most of it... So he found out I was tweaking his mind, and he went on the defensive, not even being aware of what he'd done... I had no choice but to dig directly into his soul."

The gods' spectrum of reactions to this ranged from soft chuckling to facepalming, but they all shared a common exasperation over Serelipta's actions; just as they had expected, he had no redeeming explanation.

But then, Serelipta interjected, "Could any of *you* resist looking into the soul of a human who can resist and even negate a god's power?" The gods quietly second-guessed their judgment. It was unthinkable for a human to resist a god's power at all, let alone negate it.

Serelipta continued. "There has always been some sort of anomaly within the souls of travelers from Earth. And Ryoma is quite an exceptional case, even among them. Now, I get where you're coming from here and all, but, like... Don't you think it's way too dangerous to just ignore a human who can negate our powers?"

"Hm. So you resorted to this unwarranted investigation because you saw a possible threat to us?"

"Just figured it'd help. Better safe than sorry, and all that jazz. Besides, why's it a taboo in the first place? Because gods like us interfering with mortal souls prevents them from undergoing the *natural* reincarnation that eventually happens after their death, right? But Ryoma's soul was already tampered with on his way to this world, so it's already a done deal that it'll receive special treatment after he dies. Okay, so I was a bit forceful, and he felt some pain and discomfort. But I tried to make sure there were no lasting effects. And I would've gotten away with it, too, if it weren't for that kibitzer Wilieris over there."

"Excuse me?" snarled Wilieris, goddess of the earth.

"Hey, jes' take it easy…" Grimp, the god of agriculture, stepped in to defuse the potentially dicey situation.

Gain cleared his throat. "So you are saying that you sensed a need for this investigation, and *have* kept in mind at least the bare minimum of precautions."

"Sure. I'll admit I shouldn't have gone rogue on you all. But, like, we were already on bad enough terms before circumstances forced my hand and all."

"And you think we would be on better terms if we happened to clue into your unauthorized mind control?"

"Huh…touché. Well, that's just the way the cookie crumb—"

"So? What are you hiding?"

"Huh?"

The gods stared at Serelipta hard enough to bore holes through him.

"Get real, b'y. How long d'ya think we been acquainted?"

"Much to my infinite embarrassment, we have been acquainted for an immeasurable period of time."

"You just don't mince words at all, do you?"

"The thought of an honest apology coming from your lips makes my skin crawl."

"It's just not in your design to take things on the chin, is it?"

"Yer too damn spiteful fer that."

"You always just pass the buck and don't take accountability for your actions."

Grimp, Wilieris, Kiriluel, Fernobelia, Lulutia, Tekun, and finally Kufo each gave their scathing assessments of Serelipta, as he wore a bitter expression through it all. "Guys, isn't this a bit much…?"

"Not if it's all true."

"C'mon, just spill your metaphorical guts already."

"To be fair, I don't get the feeling he's lying to us…"

"It is best that we hear the entire story before we make our decision."

"You better have had a good reason for doing this. If it turns out to be some stupid nonsense, then—"

"All right, all right! I'll tell you, okay? Sheesh!" Serelipta sighed. "Like it's gonna change much for me anyway."

"We shall decide that. Just answer the question."

"Fernobelia… Where's this attitude coming from? Like, we're equals and all, but I *am* much older than you. This whole holier-than-thou thing you got going on won't do you any favors without showing some manners."

"Yet you have broken our divine rules, and are here to be judged for it. Clearly age hasn't translated into wisdom for you, you senile old—"

"That is *quite* enough!" Gain scolded the two squabbling gods. "Fernobelia, calm yourself. And Serelipta, stop trying to distract us from the issue at hand."

"Hmph."

"Yes, sir, sorry, sir."

The mere task of keeping the gods in check had evidently taken its toll on Gain, who heaved a sigh. "I wish I could just chill out and watch an idol concert instead…"

His quiet aside went unacknowledged by the other gods.

Serelipta began again. "There's something I haven't mentioned about Ryoma, or rather, the Earth god who sent him here. Long story short, he's kind of a psycho. I found that out when I peeked into Ryoma's soul."

"Psycho?"

"Considering what Gain has told us about their actions, that does not sound surprising."

"Yeah, and I feel like this is kind of related to that… First off, have you all heard of 'life simulators'? Those are a type of game in Ryoma's world, where people enter information into a machine so they can grow mock humans, animals, or plants that aren't actually real to life."

"It sounds similar to what we are doing; watching humanity and nature evolve."

"Huh, I guess we see eye-to-eye for once, Wilieris. You're basically correct there, but there's a big difference—in these simulations, no lives or souls are involved; they just exist as blocks of information. No matter how real they might seem, not a single one of the subjects are really 'alive.' So, the player can treat them as heinously as they wish, and then just hit the reset button. That basically makes it like everything never happened. Of course, such is the difference between games and reality… But I don't think it makes any difference to the god of Earth."

"You mean they were playing a game with human lives?" Lulutia's voice quivered with stifled rage.

Serelipta gently answered, "Well, at least in Ryoma's case, yeah. You know he has all sorts of talents, Lulutia. After all, it was you who took on his reincarnation."

"Yes… Although most of those talents were wasted in his previous life."

"The ones you saw were the tip of the iceberg. Evidently, he's been given a whole slew of other talents, tucked away deep enough that nobody would figure it out unless they were to directly tap into his soul. A real wolf in sheep's clothing, you could say."

"What?!"

"Just to be clear, I'm not lying."

"Right. I suppose you wouldn't have any reason to lie to us about this. If Serelipta looked into Ryoma's soul, we'd see for ourselves... the perfect hiding place. Usually, we don't directly access a human soul without good reason."

"I see what you mean, Kufo. What talents did Earth's god go to all this trouble to hide?"

"Murder."

Serelipta's response left the other gods gobsmacked.

"Not to mention robbery, thievery, or pretty much any major crime you could think of, save for sexual violence. Guess that god didn't find those acts relevant. But yeah, most of the others were along similar lines—murder, genocide, torture. Almost as if it was beneficial for Ryoma to be specialized in the act of killing."

"Wait a minute! Are you seriously saying that the Earth god wanted to make Ryoma into a serial killer?"

"Um, I'm not finished... I'm getting to that. If you want my presumption, I think it would've been easier to make Ryoma into a violent criminal for the sake of the Earth god's goal. They wanted him to have a miserable life. Just keep all that frustration bottled up, and then one day, *snap!* You've got a killer on your hands. No turning back. Plus, Ryoma's talent for weapon handling was limited to stuff from yesteryear, like swords, bows and arrows. He couldn't handle a gun to save his life, but they made sure he'd show at least some interest in them. Maybe they wanted to see whether a master of martial arts and primitive weapons could go up

85

against guns, or see how many people he could kill. Ryoma would have been a wanted man, and he'd keep fighting back to the point that they probably would've sicced an army on him eventually. But obviously, that didn't come to pass."

Serelipta flippantly rattled off his theory, but once he finished, his expression turned serious. "But I want to be clear about one thing—Ryoma isn't a bad person."

"We are well aware of that fact."

"Indeed. Otherwise, we would have never brought him to this world."

"I agree, but what I've seen just gives me the idea that Earth's god doesn't really give a damn, so to speak, about things like that... What's your take, Fernobelia?"

"I concur. It shouldn't be too difficult to set a destiny for him and make him live out the life they want him to."

"But that's no fun, is it? If that god were to exert their power without limit, then the outcome's already a done deal. I think they were trying to beat around the bush and provide opportunities for chance, like only giving Ryoma talents and a tough environment, so they couldn't predict the outcome. Maintaining Ryoma's humanity was part of that."

"One *could* look at it in that light..."

"That's sickening..."

"At the end of the day, thanks to that game, Ryoma was able to live out his life with his free will intact. He has that ridiculously strong resistance to mind control because he fought against the temptations planted by the god of Earth. So much so that the simulation failed. There were traces of 'guiding' Ryoma, so to speak, by adding different criminal talents repeatedly, and there was some forceful destiny manipulation as well. His soul's been messed with more than a few times."

BY THE GRACE OF THE GODS

"That explains how he developed resistance to it…"

"Of course, the dear test subject has no idea of what the god was doing. He remained completely unaware of his strength, but it's impressive all the same."

Then, Grimp spoke up. "So, *that's* why ya went 'n said that."

"Uh… Seriously, Grimp?" Serelipta frowned. "You're bringing that up *now*?"

His aversion to whatever Grimp had to say further piqued the curiosity of the gods.

"Quote, 'I'm hoping you'll be truly happy, someday. Life's about to get really hectic for you, so be ready, but do enjoy your peaceful days in the little village until then. And if you really feel like you can't go on with life anymore… You know where to find me,' unquote. I ain't never heard ya's talkin' like that before, so it's been on me mind fer a while."

Serelipta sighed. "I think there were plenty of times in his previous life when he was frustrated enough with someone that he just wanted to kill them, not to mention the general temptation of crime. Still, he didn't act on those thoughts… Whether it was for selfish reasons or just all unconscious, he just put up with his lot in life until he shuffled off the mortal coil. It would've been one thing for him to just live an ordinary life, but considering how hard he fought back against the divine temptations directed at him, I kinda have to admire him for that."

"That certainly does sound impressive."

"I get that this was a game for the god of Earth, but your average mental fortitude wouldn't hold up to this. It'd take something stronger."

"Frustrating as it is, I imagine the Earth god is significantly more OP than we are…"

"Luckily for us, the god of Earth couldn't do anything with Ryoma once his soul reached our world... But his experiences were carved into his soul, and his personality was forged from those experiences. So I'm still worried about something."

Serelipta's expression grew even more pained. "If he's constantly told that he is useless by others, he'll end up believing it; no different to a child getting told the same by parents or other figures of authority. The god's little game has greatly warped the formation of Ryoma's character. Of course, some children can stay strong even as everyone around them tries to beat them down, and Ryoma would probably fit better into that category... Probably because his self-control was too strong, I guess. It must have been a self-defense mechanism to protect himself from the visceral urge to kill, because he always goes overboard when it comes to reprimanding himself or holding himself back."

"Wait...you're still talking about Ryoma, right? We've seen him taking out bandits like it was nothing."

"Yeah, and that's where it gets more complicated... He simply adapted to the law of the land there. He won't kill without a good reason, but if self-defense or food are at stake, then he won't hesitate much. That tells us something, though. You know how he gets carried away in combat? He doesn't realize it, but he's instinctively starting to sense his hidden talents and the danger they pose, and he blames himself for that."

"Wait!"

"What is it, Kufo?"

"I just remembered. Didn't Ryoma start training after parting ways with the duke's family because he went berserk in the mines?"

"Now that you mention it, yeah."

"I remember that too. But that was all down to that lowlife adventurer who tried to threaten a kid for money. Then he tried to threaten Ryoma…"

"That's true… But you know how he's become younger in this world? His mental age also regressed a bit, so that evidently softened his self-control up a little. He almost fell prey to his urges, and now he's trying to keep them in check. Killing for food when he lived in the forest and fighting bandits would have done that for sure. To be honest, I think it's pretty normal for any human to contemplate murder out of anger or some sort of grudge. It's a different story to act on that thought, let alone to feel no emotion from fulfilling it."

"So basically, Ryoma accepts that killing is sometimes necessary for survival, but he also sees that thought as abnormal and considers himself dangerous. Do we have that straight? Seems pretty contradictory."

"You're pretty close there, Fernobelia. Ryoma sees himself as a danger. That might be why he wants to join social circles, but never quite manages to fit in when he does. He feels like an outcast who doesn't belong, and doesn't deserve to belong. What's more, he feels like he has to be forgiving of others and unforgiving towards himself, that he has to always be altruistic and not ask for anything. You could say that otherwise he thinks he'd be unworthy of going on living, I suppose. A pretty strong sentiment for humans, maybe, but Ryoma follows this code too strictly; his self-esteem is just that low. That's why he accepted being treated unfairly in his previous life, and whenever someone shows him kindness, he'll try to return the favor at any cost to himself. Again, this is all unconscious."

Serelipta let out a long sigh at this point, and then started to finalize his thoughts.

"It's all well and good to be that kind of person, but doing favors for free makes him a prime target in a human society rife with greed. Some might take it as him devaluing his work. What happens when his philosophy causes him to clash with others? He could just double down on the situation, or cut his losses and run, but he's not the kind of person to do that. He's more likely to take others' criticisms deeply to heart, and try to meet a demand of theirs. He won't change the way he acts until that unconscious chink in the armor of his heart is healed. In due time, he's going to end up dealing with a lot more people than usual, and if he keeps giving a pass to all this self-inflicted psychic damage, it could very well drive him to madness. That's where I come in. I'm thinking I can take him to a deserted island, or even give him a more powerful blessing to allow him to live underwater, like the ancestors of mermaids. The farther he moves away from civilization, the easier his life would be, and even in the worst-case scenario, there would still be minimal damage to him. The human world does naturally change over time, after all. But we don't have to rush things with Ryoma either. I just figure it might be better to put him in a more laid-back area where he can gradually come to terms with himself."

"I see… You have certainly thought this over."

The other gods seemed to share Gain's sentiment as silence filled the air.

"It's certainly surprising to hear from someone who constantly told Ryoma about how uninteresting he is…"

"I meant that he's uninteresting to watch in his current circumstances. I never said I hated him, or that I wasn't interested in him at all. Besides, I try to treat every life equally; I'd do the same for anyone whether I'm interested in them or not."

Wilieris now felt quite guilty about how hard she had been on Serelipta. She was about to apologize to him, but then…

"And besides… I love humans who endure all kinds of craziness and make it out the other end in one piece."

Serelipta's comment drew flabbergasted stares from the other gods, but he continued talking excitedly without noticing.

"Like, you know what I mean, right? Kinda like the fish who gets away when the rest of their school ends up on a plate, or the one ant who gets away from an anteater unscathed. I do so love seeing a life shine brightly when it faces down death and manages to make it…out…alive?"

Serelipta finally clued into how his topic of discussion was not being particularly well-received by his audience.

"Serelipta… I swear, you are such a…"

"Who's the psycho now, huh?"

"I'd rather not have to criticize someone's worldview, but come on now."

"Maybe you could've said something more like how it reminds you of the value of life, or how you enjoy watching their valiance to survive, or even that you just enjoy supporting them?"

"And here you had me impressed for a moment."

"I sure wouldn't want to catch attention from *you*."

"B'y, ya dun goofed. Blurtin' out that crap won't do ya no favors."

"W-Wait, what's going on?"

"Serelipta." Wilieris spoke with a completely changed expression from the moment before.

"Wha— You're freaking me out! Why so angry? Where'd your sad introspection run off to?!"

"Yes, of course… Such a fool I was to think for even a second that you were worthy of reappraisal… Heh, heh heh heh…"

"I thought I was headed for acquittal on all charges for sure…"

"Such was our intention, until a minute ago. You just wanted to cloud the issue of your sentencing by talking about Ryoma so you could get away!"

"Hey, I'm not *that* insidious! I was just hoping I could get my sentence lessened by telling you all about why I treated Ryoma the way I did and what the Earth god's intentions were!"

"So you *did* have an ulterior motive!"

"Great, now she's going full Karen… Guys, help me out here!" Serelipta called to the room. "This is supposed to be a formal trial, or meeting, or whatever, right? Don't just let her turn this into a kangaroo court!"

"He has a point… I suggest we discuss this again elsewhere before we make our decision. Wilieris, I shall leave you to deal with Serelipta. Now, we shall take our leave."

"What?! Hey, Gain! Guys?!"

The gods ignored Serelipta's call and left one by one, leaving only Serelipta, still tied to his chair, and Wilieris, who was now standing directly in front of him.

"Now it's just you and I," she said.

"Uh, yeah…"

"They shall decide your punishment, but before that, you are going to hear me out. I have a *lot* to say to you, and you're going to be a good boy and accept *every! Single! Word!*"

"Ugh… Ryoma, you'll be the death of me yet…"

After a very long struggle session with Wilieris, the gods eventually returned to find Serelipta slumped over in his chair, utterly devoid of energy…

⇒ Chapter 6 Episode 27 ⇐
Interlude — Eliaria's Friends

Some time after Ryoma's departure, at a time when everyone's lives, regardless of status, became a little more animated as the new year approached, five girls were being served tea and snacks inside a capitol mansion, but only one of them had even touched them—the daughter of the manor, Eliaria.

"Girls, you needn't be so nervous. It will all work out. Kanan, feel free to indulge."

"S-So you say…"

"Kanan, with all due respect, your nervousness is rubbing off on me."

"Why?! Your father's a count, Michelle! You should be demonstrating to us what we should be doing."

"Ha! Alas, our country sort of fell into our laps as my family furthered our studies and research generation after generation. I'm not one to brag, but my parents and I would always prioritize our curiosity over etiquette. We know the bare minimum required, but nothing more. Riela should be a bit better."

"Then don't brag about it… Still, I'm not one to talk when it comes to etiquette. Should I have at least worn a dress or something?"

"We were told just to be ourselves; this is good enough. Besides, they'll see right through any airs we try to put on now."

"Really? Well, maybe you're right… You're awfully calm, Miyabi."

"Au contraire. It's more like I've…given up. I've been in a situation like this before…"

"I just want to introduce my friends to my family…"

"Elia…" Her four friends stared at her, as if to insinuate that was the very source of their nervousness.

At this point, a knock was heard from the ornately decorated door.

A maid entered and said, "Thank you for your patience. The duke has arrived."

The four friends sprang to their feet, and Elia elegantly rose to hers a beat later. Then, a young couple and an old man entered through the door.

"I regret that I kept you waiting. I am Reinhart, duke of Jamil. Thank you for spending time with my daughter."

"Father! And Mother, Grandfather… What took you so long?"

"I'm sorry, darling. We had an unexpected guest."

"You look well, Elia."

"I'm happy to see you well, Grandfather. And you as well, Mother, Father."

Once reunited, the family turned their attention to their guests.

"Could you introduce your friends to us, Elia?"

"Yes, of course! The most nervous one, over there, is Kanan."

"I am Kanan Schuzer! It is my ambition to become a crafter of magical items, my lord!"

"I see, so you are Kanan," Elia's mother answered. "Elia has written to me about you. I know of your family."

"Schuzer. How is Dufall? I used to see him often back in the day, and I was told when I visited the shop the other day that he has since retired…"

"Gramps— My grandfather is doing well. He didn't retire because he was ill, or anything of the sort. It was just his age; his eyes and fingers don't work like they used to. He simply decided to retire one day, saying that he couldn't make them like he used to…

But he's still making items every day 'as a hobby,' better than what most makers can make, and shouts the apprentices into shape… my lord."

"I'm glad to hear that. If you get a chance, please tell him that Reinbach sends his regards."

"You betcha!"

Kanan's eyes went wide at that social faux pas, but the three adults chuckled and brushed it off. While Kanan didn't realize, her constantly twitching dog ears and tail had already betrayed her nervousness and anxiety.

Without missing a beat, Elia pushed Miyabi to introduce herself.

"I'm Miyabi Saionji. As you may know, my father is Pioro, president of the Saionji company. On behalf of myself and my father, thank you for the lovely invitation, my lord."

"So you're Pioro's daughter!"

"Your father has helped our family a great deal."

"He told me he has a daughter, but I believe this is our first meeting. Pleased to make your acquaintance."

"Thank you, my lord."

"Next, we have Riela."

"Riela Clifford, my lord. Youngest daughter of Baron Clifford. It is an honor and privilege to be granted a meeting with such a gracious member of the dukedom."

"Thank you for the polite introduction. No need for formalities; we're not in public."

"I feel safer knowing you have a friend like her, Elia."

"I'd simply love to learn more about you."

"Yes, my lady! I will…do my utmost," Riela said feebly.

The adults were quietly resisting the urge to smile at her stoicism.

"Lastly, Michelle. She *is* a lady, but she wears men's clothing. Please do not get the wrong impression, Father."

"Of course. Michelle, the first daughter of Wildan, I've been told."

"An honor that you already know of me, my lord. But what mistakes could there be made about me?"

"Right. I apologize for jumping to conclusions, but… I read in one of Elia's letters that you are quite popular among female students, so…"

"You mistook her for a boy and went mad at the idea before insisting that Elia explain the matter in her next letter. Isn't that right, dear?"

"It's only natural for her to interact with the boys through the academy," Elisa's grandfather interjected. "Even if Michelle had been a boy, it's not like they were dating. You made quite a mountain out of a molehill with this; it's pitiful."

The duke seemed smaller and less impressive than he did when entering the room after these retorts from his daughter, wife, and father. However, he had succeeded in easing the nerves of the children in the room; they all seemed more relaxed now.

"Goodness, where are my manners? Please, everybody take a seat," Reinhart said.

"Do bring us some more tea, would you kindly," Elise requested of the maid.

"I've gathered some things from Elia's letters; you are all on the same team, yes?"

"Correct, my lord."

"My, that brings back memories," Elise chimed in. "I remember crawling the academy dungeon in my student years. I hope my little Elia isn't holding you back."

"On the contrary. We all have differing skill sets, so I think we're a great team. Elia is excellent at her studies, and she's the top spellcaster in our class, especially when it comes to firepower and speed. Her attacks make her an essential party member in the field."

"Swordfighting is her weakest subject, but she still always keeps up with the class, and scores highly among the girls. Kanan and I will usually take the front position, but she helps us out when we're struggling."

"She always volunteers for the little things as well. Noble-born students in the other teams tend to leave menial jobs like setting up the tent or cooking to the commoner students or their own servants. And if they have to do that sort of grunt work themselves, they often have no end of complaints about it. To be honest, we didn't even know if we should let Elia do that sort of work before we saw her plugging away at it."

After Michelle, Riela, and Kanan each gave their own testimony, the adults seemed relieved.

"Not half bad at the sword, and top of the class in magic. That's not all from the training we gave you before you started the academy. I'm proud of you, Elia."

Reinbach added, "It sounds like you have earned all this high praise, Elia. And don't concern yourself when it comes to making Elia do 'grunt work,' as you called it. At the academy, all students are treated fairly, regardless of their standing… Well, in fairness, that rule was a pure formality when I attended the academy, but we don't want to bring her up in such a way that she can't function without a servant."

"Questions of class post-graduation aside, it's a learning experience for her. I'm glad you're doing well, Elia, and that you've made such good friends."

"Mother?"

"I was worried myself, though maybe not as much as my husband here. I'm proud of my part in her discipline and education, and of the young woman she has become. But when it comes to her future in high society, well…"

"Oh…" Her friends chimed in.

"Mother! What are you telling them?!"

"She doesn't mean it in a bad way."

"Elia's nice and easy to get along with… And she treats everyone equally…"

"But she's too straight, or genuine, to play those games like all of the noble kids do."

"Yes, I know I have to entertain people like that sometimes… But all they ever do is boast about themselves. They look down on anyone of lower status, insulting their etiquette or telling them to 'know their place.' They do nothing but brag to other families of equal status and try to suck up to anyone they consider to be above them. Blowing the tiniest of things out of proportion, jumping at every opportunity to knock each other down… Almost like they're just playing a game to see who can mimic their parents the closest."

"Don't let those kids hear you say things like that, Elia. Might hit a bit too close to home."

"O-Of course. I would never say such things publicly."

"I wouldn't exactly take their side either, though."

"Much as I don't like to judge people, conversations like that are inescapable on campus. I just wish they wouldn't rope me into their affairs."

"Plus ça change… We had those circles in my time too. Contests of bragging and snide comments soon turned into a volley of insults. They'll just develop different tactics with age."

"Oh? I know plenty of adults that act their shoe size over their age. Plenty of them contribute nothing themselves, yet constantly criticize the actions of others."

"You seem to have quite a few sharp opinions yourself, my lady."

"I can tell where Elia got that from…"

"I'm just happy to see my granddaughter isn't a part of that sort of circle."

"Of course not. It's just embarrassing and immature, despite what those children might believe. Ryoma's much more like a noble in his maturity."

Michelle took notice of this comment. "Ryoma... I've heard that name before. Who is he? He is a 'he,' right?"

"Yes. You've never really talked about him, Elia."

"I've never really heard much about him either. Just that he's a friend of Elia's."

"I've been curious about that. I think she's told Miyabi a bit more than she did us. It just seemed like it was something she was enthusiastic to tell us about, so we didn't ask..."

"Oh, you haven't told them about Ryoma?" Elisa asked.

"No, I... don't believe I've explained it properly. It wasn't my intention to hide it... I just wouldn't know where to start," Elia said, to the agreement of the adults and Miyabi, who were already familiar with him. "I didn't think much of it since I didn't have any friends until I started at the academy. After getting to know my classmates and other students in the grades above me, I started to realize that Ryoma was quite different from most people his age, in terms of his mental faculties. But he's not a bad person... He's very nice, in fact. Isn't he?"

"Yes. I was the first in my family to meet him. One of my men had been injured, and Ryoma saved his life."

"He told us he was raised by his grandparents, who were both adventurers. He's a year younger than Elia, but very knowledgeable and a good hunter."

"And decent at magic too, though his spells were focused on improving the quality of life."

"He must be a very talented boy. Of course, he's only a year younger than any of us."

"Talented... Yes, indeed."

"He can also be a little unusual sometimes."

"Unusual?"

"Ryoma studies slimes as a hobby. He talks about them the way you talk about magic circles, Michelle."

"Ah..." That was all it took for Riela and Kanan to get a grasp on Ryoma's character.

"Why are you dragging me into this?"

"The comparison was apt."

"Indeed. It's easy to see that he's also the type of person who has blinders on to everything except his particular interest."

Michelle grumbled to herself.

"It also goes for both of you that you are very knowledgeable about your interests and many other things. Just as Ryoma helped me catch a slime for my first familiar, you've taught me everything I know about magic circles, Michelle."

"Fine... I'm not exactly flattered, but I can live with that. That explains why you have three rare slimes with you, Elia."

"Cleaner, healer, and scavenger respectively, yes? They're terribly convenient. We got some jealous looks during camping drills at the academy dungeon."

"We had a simple bathroom and an actual bath, thanks to Elia's slime and Michelle's earth magic. Not even the teachers had it that good."

"Which put me, the negotiator of the team, in a tough situation once those nobles demanded we hand it over, or make them their own facilities..."

"That was quite the fiasco..."

"The first drill is always rough, every year. I'm sure most students cover the basics before entering the academy, but you only acquire skills by practicing them over and over again."

"One can only hope for allies who can share the workload and cover each other's weakness... Nowadays, too many adults, let alone children, conflate mere selfishness with living honorably as a noble..."

"Now that I think about it..." Elia continued telling tales of things that had happened in the academy, and her friends gradually warmed up to her stories. Eventually, the sun began to sink into the horizon.

"Excuse me. My lord, your appointment is due."

"Is it time already?"

"Father, you mean to say you had other plans when you knew I was bringing friends over?"

"I'm sorry, Elia. I'm meeting a schoolmate for dinner, one whom I haven't seen in some time."

"Father...?"

"What's the matter? You look positively astonished."

"You...had friends in school?" The question froze the air of the cozy room, replacing it with palpable tension.

Reinhart's face twitched at the remark. "Wh-Why would you say that?"

"Well... You've never gone to visit a friend before, and you always seem so unhappy when you speak of your time at the academy."

"Right, well..." Stumped, Reinhart turned to his wife and father but was only met with stifled laughter. Reinhart sighed, knowing he had to bear this burden himself. "I don't enjoy admitting it, but my school days were not much fun for me. Still, I had a friend or two whom I could trust. Take Elise, for example. We were good friends long before we decided to marry."

Elise giggled. "Now *that* most certainly brings back memories."

"I didn't know… I'm sorry, Father."

"Don't apologize. You make it sound like you're pitying me… Don't worry about it. I do visit my friends from time to time; I just haven't seen the friend I'm seeing tonight in a long time."

"Then why now…?"

"I've heard that Ryoma visited his land some time ago and discovered that, despite our status as nobles and our professional differences, my friend still cared about me. I figured today would be a good day to pay him a visit."

"I see…"

"He was quite surprised to hear from me, apparently. It's a lucky thing to have a friend who's still trying to help you after so many years. I'm hoping that you'll make a friend like that, Elia. You don't need too many of them; just one will do."

"Yes, Father. But don't worry about that!" Elia declared and looked over her four friends. "I have four friends like that right here, and five if I include Ryoma!"

"Elia…"

"Now that's the spirit."

"Straight to the point…"

"Sheesh, now I'm getting bashful."

"Oh… Perchance, you all didn't really want to be my friends?" Elia asked, and the four reassured Elia, laughing.

The adults warmly smiled at the children.

"I'm really happy to see this. You were already lucky enough to meet these friends, Elia. I'm really sorry I can't stay and hear more stories, but I must be going. Please, stay as long as you like."

"Yes, I'd love to hear more stories," Elise said. "Why don't you all stay the night? I wanted to discuss the gown for Elia's next party anyway. And not only that, we just received new samples of Ryoma's beauty products. He was quite adamant that we give *very* detailed feedback. Would you care to indulge?"

"Ryoma sent you beauty products?"

"We made a little deal a while back. I won't deny my own interest in them, but he said something about how it was relevant to his study of medicine, something he'd already learned the basics of from his grandmother. He's always been very studious. Confidentially, these beauty products of his are not only simple to use, but of quite high quality as well."

"Interesting… My mother studies medicine as well, actually…"

With the atmosphere in the room seemingly rekindled, the girls kept chattering away merrily into the night.

⌁ Chapter 6 Episode 28 ⌁
Interlude — Reinhart and Porco

One cold night in the noble district of the capital, where glamorous manors stood in rows, the duke Reinhart was visiting a relatively small and drab estate that belonged to a man he was once close to.

"Welcome, Duke Jamil. Although I've seen you at the annual balls, I believe it's been some time since we've spoken in private."

"Indeed. Though we had many a conversation as students together, of course. I would like to call you Porco, like the good old days. So please feel free to drop the formalities."

"I... Very well, then."

Their conversation continued in the foyer, still underlined with lingering formality.

"It was kind of like this when we first met, actually," started Reinhart.

"Right. I didn't think anyone would show up there, least of all the talk of the academy."

"I couldn't exactly build a relationship with anyone I wished, as it would have hindered my father."

"Not even His Majesty could ignore your influence. Not because of your father, but because of his contract with a divine beast. I'm sure plenty of kids came up to you under their parents' orders. Not that I blame them either."

"Oh, that reminds me, Porco. I saw my daughter for the first time in a while before I came here. I asked her to bring a friend because I was curious about how academy life was treating her, and she brought four; all wonderful children."

"Splendid. Why do you sound so unhappy about it?"

"On my way out, I mentioned that I was coming here, and she said she didn't know I had friends in the academy."

"Tough break… You haven't told her?"

"I've told her enough for her to be aware. Of course, I don't want her to feel the same way I did. She doesn't have many nobles of her same age in our circle… And honestly, I feel that made her a more honest and genuine young lady, which I'm proud of."

"Not to sound flippant, but I hope that doesn't come back to bite you on the ass."

"Of course I'm ready to jump in if needed, but it's important for them to live through the experience themselves. And she's already made five close friends in less than a year, when it took me six years to make just one friend. I hope they'll be of great support to her."

"Five? Would the fifth happen to be…"

"Yes, it's Ryoma. I heard you gave him quite the warm welcome. I wanted to thank you for that."

"I hardly did very much. In fact, he was the one who helped me. I thanked him the best I could."

"So I've heard. He received quite a remarkable reward."

Porco couldn't help but raise his eyebrow at Reinhart's comment. "Hm. Was it unsatisfactory? Unfortunately, I could not repay him with any more than that…"

"No, neither of us took issue with it. He actually thinks you were much too generous… It's just not the same, is it?" Reinhart asked.

Porco answered slowly but honestly. "To tell the truth… I appreciate you wanting to leave our titles at the door, and for seeking me out as a schoolmate. I really do, but… I think I've grown too old to take your offer at face value."

"I understand. We each have responsibilities that come with our title. And, while it's true that I want to speak with you as old friends, that isn't the only reason why I'm here… No sense in beating around the bush anymore. Shall we take care of business first?"

"I would appreciate that."

"Then let me be blunt, Porco. I would like to attend these meetings you're hosting."

"Do you mean the dinners I host as a hobby…? What makes you want to attend?"

"I heard from Ryoma that you've been told rumors of unsavory incidents in my land."

"I have… Don't tell me."

"Regrettably, it seems that there are several clans in cahoots orchestrating them."

Porco covered his eyes. "Who are those idiots…? Sounds like you already have a good idea. Which means you're not looking for help in resolving your current problems, I presume."

"I appreciate that you always move our conversations along. I don't like playing games or fighting for power, so I want them to understand what happens to those who mess with my family and my people while making new connections to prevent this from happening again."

"There would be plenty of families itching to befriend the duke without my help."

"That's true, but I don't want to befriend any old noble. It would mean a lot if you could help me, Porco. You've always been thorough and careful, not to mention that you're keeping up with these connections through your dinners… I'll repay you for your troubles, of course; my men are waiting outside with your recompense."

"I'll have them brought in." Porco rang a bell on his desk, and Pigu entered the room.

Once Porco gave his orders, the butler swiftly brought in three boxes of varying sizes.

"Take a look at this first." Reinhart handed him a thin, rectangular box.

"A necklace…?" Porco guessed from the shape of the box. While he was correct, what rested inside the box was more than what he had imagined. "Pearls?! A whole string of them, even, and the sizes are all equal."

In this landlocked country, even a single pearl was incredibly valuable. Porco couldn't even imagine how much he would have to pay to acquire a full necklace of them.

"It's breathtaking. What else is there to say...?" Porco carefully returned the box and asked, "What's the point in showing me this? It's far too extravagant for me. Don't tell me that's the repayment you spoke of?"

"If you want one, Porco, I can get another one just like it. As for this particular one, though, I plan to gift it to an acquaintance. He just got married last year, and he's been looking far and wide for a gift for his wife."

"An acquaintance who married last year, receiving something like this... So it's meant for His Majesty, then. You must be looking for a permit to sell pearls in return."

"Many nobles want access to pearls. I don't know how you got these, but if you can so easily prepare another necklace like this one... With His Majesty's seal of approval, you'll gain significant influence, not to mention your income. A connection to the duke of pearls... Were I to take that role, I would gain some voice and influence myself. Of course, I'd expect to make some new enemies along the way."

"To a certain degree, yes. But my family will back you up. I don't want you to be a mere cushion between my family and the other nobles, but a partner who can support others and be supported in turn. In part, this is because you're already involved in my sourcing of these pearls."

"What?"

"Take a look at these," Reinhart said, and opened another box to reveal some shells, their well-polished nacre brilliantly shining.

"This sheen... But that shape—"

111

"Ryoma found them in your land, Porco. I've heard they are shells common to those areas."

"These are sandrills, then."

"You asked him to clean a hot spring? He apparently used the cleaner he concocted for the job to polish these."

"That cleaner! I never knew there was such brilliance hidden beneath the surface of these shells."

"From what he's told me, the shells are made from the same material as pearls... I want you to provide these shells, labeled for consumption."

"Since you're seeking them out, I assume the shells are made into those pearls."

"To be precise, other materials, the grime that Ryoma cleaned from the hot spring, for example, can be substituted for them, but these shells would be the best option as the long-term supply."

"Did the thought of being more subtle about it not cross your mind?"

"I wanted to be frank with you, and I didn't want to waste our time. You will help me, won't you, Porco?" Reinhart asked with full confidence.

Porco, either from exasperation or resignation, leaned all the way back into his chair and gazed up at the ceiling.

"This is a good deal for me as well. Besides, would you even take no for an answer?"

"I could deal with a refusal if you were insistent about it. But the deal with the shells was something Ryoma asked me to bring to you in the first place."

"What?"

"These shells were harvested in your land, so he thought you should know about it. That being said, he was concerned that making you aware of these shells in such a manner might have caused you trouble or invited suspicion. It didn't seem like he knew much about your troubles, but he had suspected that you had a delicate matter at hand, from what he had heard during his stay. So, he asked me for a favor. Just to be clear, his intentions for telling you this are completely innocent. I'm not trying to force you to do anything in exchange for your information. I have a lot more to lose by disappointing Ryoma."

"Ah. I always knew he wasn't an ordinary child, but I didn't think he'd see through me that easily."

"At first, both my wife and I were worried about him. He seemed sheltered and gullible, but it seems he can be quite perceptive."

Watching Reinhart speak of Ryoma, Porco's reservations seemed to begin to melt.

"Don't tell me he's your bastard son, Reinhart."

Porco's unexpected comment made Reinhart choke on the tea he'd been sipping. "What the devil put *that* idea into your head?"

"You had this look on your face... Bittersweet, like you've just realized how much your child has grown."

"I made such a face?"

"You didn't notice?"

"Does it matter? He is not my offspring, legitimate or otherwise."

"There's no outward resemblance, of course, but I see some of your tendencies in him."

"Well, enough joking around. Let's get back on track."

"You're the one who wanted to talk with me like in the good old times... All right, all right. Please stop giving me that ominous smile; it's unsettling. Where were we?"

"Ryoma had asked me to tell you about these shells, and that he's rather perceptive. If these shells see the light of day, the struggle for rights over Lake Latoin will scarcely remain under the surface but turn into a full-out brawl."

"Absolutely. It's unfortunate that many in my land would spring for such selfish, short-term gains."

"Your father paving those roads must have had a lot to do with it, but where it used to be nearly uninhabitable, save for the settlements around the lake, your land has improved drastically, and could be made even better. I believe it is steadily becoming a highly attractive landscape."

"Couldn't have been a better time to gain the support of a duke, to be honest. I can ensure you are invited to every dinner party, as well as full support with introducing you to as many other powerful nobles as I can."

They shook hands.

"What's in the third box, anyway?"

"Another potential win-win. Can you help me with it?"

"I thought I'd seen all of the surprises you've packed for the day... No need to waste our time, right? Tell me what you need."

"Would you be interested in a new technology that preserves food for longer while maintaining its taste and freshness?"

"Of course; my main export is fresh fish, after all."

"That technology is currently in testing. The box contains a prototype of a food-freezing magical item."

"Freezing food negatively affects flavor. Is there a way around that?"

"The food stays much fresher compared to traditional freezing. I think it's market ready as-is."

"How does it work?"

"Apparently, the key is in rapidly freezing the food at a much lower temperature than most magical items allow. A very strong liquor called industrial alcohol is used to achieve this. I've heard that there is a local drink called white ale in Fatoma, that most people can make themselves."

"There is. It takes a certain amount of time and skill to make it palatable, but the taste wouldn't matter if it would just serve as a base for this alcohol. The ingredients for it grow in the wild, and it wouldn't be hard to farm if need be. That's why you're telling me this deal." Porco nodded to himself before adding, "Reinhart. I feel a sense of déjà vu. I keep seeing a certain boy behind this invention."

"You've guessed right. This is another one of Ryoma's experiments."

"How does he keep inventing all these things?"

"With our partnership established, I suppose I should tell you... He was raised by the famous sage Meria and the warrior Tigral, but they were not related by blood."

"A traveling bard had dubbed him the Barley Tea Sage. Perhaps the moniker's more fitting than it seemed." Porco cracked a smile at this revelation, before readopting his stoic expression. "I might as well say this now—I think the boy needs to be more careful."

"You think so too...?" Reinhart's expression hardened. "There have always been signs, but what happened this time made it clear to me. He's a bit too altruistic."

"I'm sure he's told you, but I asked him to do a few jobs for me. He delivered exceptional results in both cases, but had no interest at all in his reward."

"That's only a symptom of the bigger issue."

"What do you mean?"

"The problem is something more at the core of his humanity. That's what I think."

"Did something happen which made you think that?"

"Yes. Nonetheless, I— My family and I will continue to support him, both publicly and personally."

Seeing the burning resolve in Reinhart's eyes, Porco regained his smile. "You haven't changed at all."

"D-Do you think so?"

"Not one bit... Very well! Let's talk over all of it, shall we? Eat, drink, be merry, and complain about the woes of our jobs and raising children. What else are friends for?"

"Thank you, Porco..."

"No need for that. We'll be working together now, like the good old days."

Porco rang the bell once more and ordered Pigu to rush their dinner out. Then, Porco and Reinhart continued their conversation, beginning to rekindle their friendship.

～ **Chapter 7 Episode 1** ～
The Changes in Gimul

"It feels different here, somehow…"

After carriage-hopping from Fatoma, I had safely arrived in Gimul. Given I hadn't set foot in this town for a whole month, my feelings of nostalgia were dwarfed by a sense of unease; even with a greater pedestrian presence on the streets, the town seemed quite dilapidated.

"Stop right there!" I heard a shout as I was making my way to the shop. Turning towards the voice, I saw three guards chasing after a man. *Must be a purse-snatcher or something.*

One of the guards, being quicker on his legs, soon caught up to the man. "I've got you now!"

"Let go of me, you fu—!"

"Look out!"

"Whoa!"

"Suck on this, asshole!"

The guards failed to completely restrain the perp, allowing him to draw a knife and flail it around, injuring the first guard's face and making him loosen his grip.

"He's getting away!"

"Get him!"

The third guard soon caught up with the criminal and managed to restrain and apprehend him.

"Are you all right?!"

The injured guard groaned in response. While his injury didn't seem life-threatening, he was bleeding quite a bit. I wondered if they would let me heal it with my magic.

"Excuse me," I called to the injured guard.

"What do you want?! This is a serious situation!"

"I happen to know healing magic. Maybe I could help with that wound, if you don't mind?"

"Healing... Pardon me, that would be much appreciated!"

With his permission, I took a closer look at the wound and cast an intermediate High Heal. The wound wasn't as deep as the bleeding suggested, so just one cast did the trick.

"How do you feel? Any discomfort?"

"I'm fine now. No pain at all."

"Terrific."

Seeing the guard healed, one of the other guards said to me, "I appreciate your help, young man. I must apologize for my behavior just now."

"Hey, it's fine. Your colleague got hurt and all, I get it."

"No, injuries are part of the job, and something we must be prepared to accept. It's inexcusable that I've raised my voice against one of the citizens we are meant to protect, let alone a kind young man who volunteered to heal us. I've had a long day, but I must still apologize for that shameful display," he reiterated. He definitely took his job very seriously.

"I said it's fine... Anyway, would you mind if I ask a few questions?" I explained how I had been away from the city for a bit, and asked about the changes I've noticed.

"Did you see the new town being built south of here?"

"Yes. While I've only seen the exterior walls, they've made a lot of progress."

"That's all well and good, but people looking for a job in the construction have filled our streets… Look over there." He pointed towards the alleys, where there were people sitting or laying down on the ground. There was one man who had been digging in the trash behind a restaurant, now being chased away by the owner.

"I'm surprised there are so many of them so close to the main road."

"The population was already on the rise a month ago, but it wasn't this bad. The number of workers coming in has far exceeded our expectations. Now street crimes and fights are a lot more common. We've tried to deal with it by hiring more staff, but even with all our under-trained rookies on the job, we're still having to pull overtime."

With renewed respect and gratitude for the guards, I said, "Well, thanks for taking the time to talk with me. I know you're busy and all, keeping everybody safe and stuff. Thanks a lot for your service."

"I appreciate it. Be careful out there, and try to get home before night falls."

I bid the guards farewell and went back on my way to the shop.

■　■　■

When I arrived, I tried to enter through the back door when a man I didn't recognize stopped me. "Identify yourself. Nobody gets past this door unless they're an employee."

While I was curious about who he was, I explained my identity to him and asked to see Carme. He must have been told about me beforehand, because he quickly changed his tone.

"Welcome back, Chief!" he said, as he let me in without further argument. "Sorry about that. I'd heard our boss was a kid, but I thought they were having a laugh. Figured you'd be in your late teens or something."

"Yeah, I guess that'd be easier to believe."

With that misunderstanding settled, the now-friendly man introduced himself as Hudom. He was a blonde human in his twenties, with a bit of a surfer vibe to him. He had introduced himself as a martial artist, and he was well-built, but more in a toned boxer way than a bodybuilder way. He had been traveling the country to test his mettle, when he stopped by Gimul and happened to come across Chelma, the chef, being accosted by some ruffians, and helped Chelma get back to the shop safely. Once that story was shared in the shop, Carme decided to increase the shop's security. After discussing it with Ox and Fay, he offered Hudom a temp job as a security guard.

"Thank you for keeping the shop safe, Carme. And thank you for helping us out, Hudom."

"I endeavor to earn my pay," Carme answered.

"I was running out of funds, so it was good timing for me too. I get good perks. The shop is nice. And I get endless opportunities to test my strength. It's a great gig for me."

"I'm glad to hear that."

"I heard you're quite the fighter yourself, Chief... Yeah, you look legit to me. Want to spar?"

Wait, what?

"Is something wrong?" he asked.

"I've been told I don't look like a fighter. I'm just rather surprised you'd make me such an offer."

"Right. I guess you couldn't tell at a glance, but I was paying close attention out there before I figured out who you were. I've challenged a good number of dojos too. Your stride definitely betrays your hidden strength."

He certainly sounded like he knew his stuff, so he made me feel safer about the shop with his obsession.

"I've been a bit concerned. The city's changed since I was last here... How is everyone else doing, Carme?"

"Well, with Hudom's addition, I do feel safe about the shop, and everyone is able to do their jobs without worrying about their safety. That being said, we do need to shop for supplies and the like, so we're concerned about the rise in crime."

"Just the other day, there was an arson at the Morgan Trading Company."

"What? At Serge's place?"

Carme nodded. He and his sister Carla came to me from the Morgan Trading Company, bringing word from Serge. It could not have been easy for them to hear that someone had tried to burn down their old stomping grounds.

"The fire was quickly extinguished, thanks to the company having hired evening security. It was a brazen attempt by several perpetrators, who threw pots of oil into the building and ignited them with fire magic. They escaped in the commotion and are still at large. Security was hardly lax, so they assumed the arsonists knew what they were doing and that the attack was premeditated… It was a very big deal."

"Sure sounds like it."

The Morgan Trading Company was one of those famous brands that everyone knew. They had earned reputation and trust among consumers over the years. Furthermore, their Gimul location was their headquarters, where many people patronized them, even those who didn't know for sure where it was in the city. Had a crime of comparable scale occurred on Earth, it would be blasted at everyone within earshot of a news media network for weeks.

"How is Serge?"

"Unharmed, for a start. Security was directed to protect the employees first and foremost, so there were no injuries or casualties."

"Glad to hear it." Still, this topic, along with the changing city, was something I was eager to discuss. "Carme. Is there anything here that needs urgent attention?"

"A few documents that need your approval, but those can wait until tomorrow. You must be tired after such a long journey."

"Thank you. I'll take my leave for the day, then. I acquired a few things in Fatoma, so I'd like to stop by Serge's."

"Understood. Please give him my regards."

"Speaking of, I also brought something for everyone, so I'll bring those by tomorrow. See you then!"

With barely any time to settle in, I hurried out of the shop and headed towards the Morgan Trading Company.

～ **Chapter 7 Episode 2** ～
Inspiration and a Meeting with Serge

Leaving Carme in charge of the shop, I headed straight for Serge's.

When I arrived, I found a vast scorch mark across the exterior of the welcoming wooden storefront. In front of it stood a few men of intimidating stature and wearing similarly intimidating expressions. Over half a year had passed since my arrival in Gimul, but I'd never felt so tense here before. When I first came to the city, it had been such a welcoming place. I felt like I'd lost something, imagining that the current state of Serge's shop was representative of the entire city.

"Excuse me. Have you any business here?"

I snapped out of my thoughts; evidently, I'd been standing around longer than I realized. "Oh, yes! I'm friends with the president. I was out of town for a bit, and heard about the arson as soon as I returned. I don't have an appointment, because I came here in a hurry."

The man who called me gave a look to one of the other men in formation, who went into the shop.

"Please wait here for a moment while we verify that information."

"Yes, thank you."

A few minutes later, I found myself in the familiar meeting room. Serge entered after some time, looking tired but in good spirits.

"Master Ryoma. I believe we last saw each other at the duke's manor."

"It's been too long. I'm sorry to hear about the fire, but I'm glad to see you're unhurt."

"I apologize for causing undue worry, but as you can see, I am doing fine. I've ramped up my security detail quite a bit as well."

"So I saw. They're a lot more polite than they look."

"They're mercenaries from the capital. You may imagine all mercenaries to be ruffians, but top-class professionals are courteous and well-mannered. Unlike adventurers, who are required to deal with varying enemies from humans to monsters in diverse environments, mercenaries are specialized in dealing with human conflict. They're expected to not offend their clients, at the very least. Trusted mercenaries even take on negotiating with the enemy, if needed."

Interesting... I guess higher-level mercs have a more diplomatic side to them.

"And lest we forget, this city is in a state where we need people like them."

"Unfortunately, yes. Arson, like what happened to my shop, is merely one of the issues; assaults and burglaries seem to be on the rise. Do you have any idea why?"

"I've been told it's something to do with too many workers coming into the city, so the number of people who are employed but homeless has exploded. But has that really driven the crime rate up this much?"

"The local government and guild are trying to mitigate the issue, of course. They've tried cutting off calls for workers, for example. But trying to stop the tide has been a losing game. There are even some con artists who pretend to be a hiring manager for the project here; they'll charge these prospective workers a fee before ditching them right outside the city. This isn't something I would mention in public, but... This phenomenon seems to have been manufactured by a few different nobles."

"You mean—?!"

"Sabotage against the duke, surely. I have no clue as to their motive, only that it must be something foolish. I've found out through offering my assistance that Duke Reinhart is already moving to get to the bottom of all of this and put an end to it."

"Really?"

"Crime is up now, but it should settle down in time. Until then, we're playing the waiting game and keeping ourselves safe."

"Great idea."

I guess if they already know that much, they just have to keep their defenses up and just wait out the storm for now...

"I understand you've brought me something, Master Ryoma?"

"Oh, that's right! As you know, I went to Fatoma for an adventurer gig. I happened to get lucky while there, so I decided to play the part of a buyer. I'd like to show you what I bought, and a new kind of product as well."

"You certainly have my interest. So, what have you brought?"

From my Item Box, I produced each of the pieces of pottery I had bought in Fatoma.

"A bowl, a mug, a cooking pot, a jar, and a plate... These all look great for daily use; the quality seems quite good. How many of these do you have?"

"Here." I handed him a list I had written up when I purchased them all.

"Hm... In that case, I can offer you about this much. I can't pay a premium for any of them, but you've picked some safe options."

"I took advice from the seller," I admitted. Serge had offered me a sum that was about twenty percent more than what I'd paid. Hardly a massive profit, but it was enough to cover my travel expenses and still leave me some spending money; not bad for a side hustle I'd pulled on my way home from another job.

"That price works for me."

"Terrific."

Then, I produced the pot Lord Fatoma had given me as a token of his thanks. Judging by how the shopkeeper had acted, and by how carefully it was wrapped, I was planning to display it in my shop, but I wanted to get an accurate estimate of its value first. I explained all of this to Serge, and he started to inspect the item.

"G-Goodness me..."

Serge's expression turned quite stern when he opened the box the pot was kept in. He quickly produced a pair of white gloves from his pocket and slipped his hands into them, then carefully unwrapped the pot. He gently placed it on the table; the pot had a bluish-white hue with ornate, vibrant patterns. It looked like quite an artisanal piece to me...

"Hrm..."

"Uh, is it an impressive piece?"

"From the blue tint and the vibrant details, this is most likely a find from an ancient ruin."

"An ancient ruin?"

"A relic of an ancient civilization said to have had advanced technologies. A few of them have been excavated at various locations around the world; I recall that one had been found in Fatoma long ago. This pot is a very valuable art piece, but its method of production was lost to time, so there is no modern equivalent. Pieces that are in such a pristine condition are extremely rare, giving it historical value as well... I don't think I can accurately appraise this. If that's what you're looking for, I suggest taking it to a specialist."

"Why would Lord Fatoma give such an important piece to me?"

"I wouldn't know… But if it was given to you as a reward for a quest, I assume he valued your work as much as this piece. What did you do for this lord?"

Well, I didn't tell Lord Fatoma about the pearls or those shells… I ended up telling Serge about cleaning the hot springs, my modest gyoza proposal, and how to properly prepare poisonous fish.

"I see. Lord Fatoma is famous for his culinary passion, and I hear he has a large circle of like-minded friends. He would be interested in any new intel to do with food, and I suppose he's confident he can make good use of it. If the economy in Fatoma were to improve thanks to your introduction of the gyoza dish, benefiting his land for decades to come… This pot would be a fitting reward, to say the least."

Really…? I'll definitely have to handle this thing delicately. If I were going to display it, I'd need some kind of dedicated, protective case for it.

"Let's move on to my slime products."

"A new line of slime products? This does have me interested."

I displayed the acidic cleaner I had used at the hot spring, with a spool of string next to it. Serge's interest was clearly more piqued by the string.

"This acidic cleaner is a product of a sticky slime solution and acid slime acid. It has to be handled with caution, but it can be used for certain types of grime; around the bathroom, for example."

"I expect there would be some demand for this in the household, but especially in the likes of inns. It depends on its method of use and the caution required, I suppose. What is this string? It's clearly different from the sticky slime string."

As I figured he would, Serge steered the conversation towards the string. "This was made by a slime that evolved on my way home from Fatoma."

"What kind of slime is it?"

It was a fiber slime, evolved from a sticky slime that ate the seines in Fatoma. If I had to assume from its name, it could have evolved from any source of fiber. Even before its evolution, this particular sticky slime had a tendency towards spewing string, and I had often asked it to make the string I was selling to the Morgan company; I wondered if that had anything to do with its evolution. The only other change it underwent through evolution was the acquisition of a skill called Fiberfy.

"Apparently, the Fiberfy skill allows it to melt down materials it ingests before reshaping it like string and spewing it out."

When I first figured out what this skill did, I was reminded of rayon from my previous life. Rayon—also known as artificial silk—was created by melting cellulose, the main component of plant material, with an alkaline solution before spinning it into fibers. While the fiber slime's fiber skill didn't use any chemicals, the process was similar to that of rayon manufacturing. After that discovery, I began feeding the fiber slime cellulose. Eventually, I tried giving it shed skin from fluff slimes, which led to the manufacturing of this particular string composed entirely of slime parts.

"I call it slime rayon! I can't mass-produce it with just the one fiber slime, but I have more than enough fluff slime sheddings to go around, and I could always feed them more fertilizer if I need more materials. Would you consider putting it on your shelves?"

"This is fantastic! The sheen, the texture… It's slightly different from silk, but extremely similar. I can only imagine what splendid fabric you can weave with this. Between the ease of ordering and its high quality, this would be quite a boon indeed."

Organic silk was made out of silkworm cocoons, so there was only so much that could be harvested within the season. Slime rayon, on the other hand, could be produced any time I wished by giving the fiber slime the necessary ingredients. As the fiber slime split and multiplied, productivity would rise too.

"This would allow me to continue to provide traditional silk products to nobles, and faux silk products for other customers."

"It's difficult to start fresh in an established market, though."

"Precisely. And if we can establish that line between real and faux silk products, the nobles will rush to acquire the genuine stuff; we wouldn't get on the wrong side of silk dealers or producers. We would need more productivity to sell it to the public, but it looks like that will come in due time. Do you mind if I hold onto this spool?"

"Yes, I would love for you to look into its potential."

"Understood."

The slime rayon business could very well blow up, big time. I had one more piece to discuss, though. "Oh, Serge..."

"You sound like you're about to bring out something really impressive."

"Yes. It's another product which I'm able to produce now, thanks to one of my slimes having evolved. I was taken completely by surprise, to be honest. This will be more valuable than anything I've shown you before."

"That means a lot coming from you, Master Ryoma... I'm ready," Serge said, giving me the same look he had when I talked about the blood slime serums.

I placed the small box before him. It was, I dare say, the pièce de résistance of my trip—the small box of pearls. The moment he saw it, Serge slumped into his chair like he was having a heart attack.

"Serge, are you all right?!"

He waved me off, apparently to show that he was okay, but he was muttering something, as if he was performing calculations.

It took several minutes for him to return to normal. "I apologize for that display," he finally said.

"No, I'm sorry to have surprised you."

"You certainly *did* surprise me." Serge nodded. "These are most definitely pearls. Just one would not have surprised me so, but you said you can *produce* these?"

"I can. A newly evolved slime of mine has a pearl body, and it learned a skill that produces pearls. I wouldn't go telling that to everyone, obviously. You're the first person aside from me to know."

"That's a relief…"

"How much do pearls go for, anyway? I only know that they're extremely expensive since they can't be found in this country."

"Even a single pearl like this would cost at least a small platinum coin. Market value, that is."

If I remember correctly, that's ridiculously expensive—a million sutes.

"That much?" I asked.

"There are many factors that drive up the price. First, the process of hunting pearls in the ocean is very dangerous because of sea monsters. Another is the low chance of finding a pearl in the harvested shells—about one in tens of thousands. Furthermore, their shape and coloration are completely unpredictable, making only a small portion of them suitable for jewelry, driving the costs up even further… They can still be acquired relatively cheaply in their country of origin, though. We are far from the only country without any access to pearls. Merchants flock to those countries and fight over what little supply there is. Through the process of exporting the pearls, plus paying for taxes, transport, and other costs for the journey, the prices of the pearls skyrocket. The merchants need to make a profit too, after all. The price will fluctuate based on the catch of the season, as well. A small platinum coin per pearl is more of a minimum…"

131

Serge nattered on with a lot more fire in his voice than I was used to. *So basically, they're super valuable.*

"If they're that valuable, then…"

"Master Ryoma?"

Something came to my mind, like an inspiration. Information lit up my synapses, and even things that seemed unrelated before seemed to all come together.

"Is something the matter, Master Ryoma?"

"Serge."

"Yes…?"

"Do you remember the discussion we had about processing trash?"

"Processing trash… The one where you proposed using scavenger slimes to take care of the city's trash? Yes, I do remember that."

"During my stay at the village in Fatoma, I was given household trash almost every day. In addition to feeding the scavenger slimes, they helped me find different evolutions for other slimes, like the fiber slime, which resulted from trash produced by different lifestyles. When I gathered the trash from all over the village, there was a lot of trash that helped speed up the evolution process. I believe collecting trash would be a very beneficial endeavor for me."

"R-Right… I suppose that makes sense."

"It makes a lot of sense. So hear me out: I want to build a trash-processing plant, solely for my own benefit. Though the scavengers can process all of the trash, I need a lot more hands for a project like this. People to collect the trash, people to sort out the materials necessary for evolutions and experiments, people to manage those people… Most positions would require manual labor, so I always thought it would be a challenge to find employees… But now—"

"The streets are full of people looking for work…!"

"Exactly. Couldn't I hire as many people as I wanted, and be as picky as I liked in the selection process? I don't know what those nobles behind these incidents are thinking, but I'm sure there are a good number of people who came to Gimul looking for work in good faith; there's got to be a few skilled workers around. Moreover, people desperate for a job are willing to accept less from their employers. I wouldn't want to criminally underpay them or give them a poor work environment... But if you're an employer, this town is your oyster right now."

"There are definitely some people who place too much value in their abilities... I see what you're getting at."

"And of course, there's the matter of this." I indicated the box on the table. "I would need funds to start a new business and to hire staff for it. Of course, it would be ideal to cover those costs through the business itself."

"Even if you don't make a profit right away, selling these pearls would certainly hold you over for a while."

"My thoughts exactly. There are a lot of things that I'd like to... no, that I need to do." For a start, I had to protect the shop from the current state of the city. At the same time, I had to continue preparing for my journey into the Sea of Trees of Syrus; specifically, I needed to train myself and study medicine and healing in case push came to shove. I'd also probably want to study tools and preserved food to make my life easier, not to mention study slimes, of course.

With my ever-increasing slime population, I wanted to utilize the monster used as feed for other monsters, the ones I was told about at Reinhart's, but I apparently had to take an exam at the tamers' guild in order to earn a permit to possess them.

There were already so many things on my plate that I was barely getting enough time to keep up with my slime studies. If I were to add any more, I wouldn't get anything done. And who knew how long it would take me if I waited until I'd finished everything to go to the Sea of Trees? I'd considered just going there, but I didn't want to be caught unprepared.

"But you and the team have always told me that I don't need to do it all alone."

"Indeed we have. Quite often, at that."

"Well, you definitely have a point. I want to research slimes on my own, but I can look for people to delegate studying preserved food and tool crafting to. Right?"

"I trust you, Master Ryoma… But aren't you simply trying to provide those workers with jobs?"

"What do you mean? That would be a task for the government or the nobles, or whoever. I can't do something like that on my own; it's a mug's game. I'm just trying to use this fortune that fell into my lap for my own benefit, to further my hobby and block out more time in my life for it. It's all very self-serving, I promise. Of course, I do think there will be more jobs to go around as a result."

"Now I'm not so sure I trust you."

Serge stared at me. I had no idea why I was being placed under such scrutiny.

Soon, Serge let out a sigh, seeming convinced. "Very well. There's some groundwork to lay out, as with any new business, but especially with something like trash processing. Let's discuss the details at the Merchant's Guild with the guildmaster in attendance. What do you say?"

"Thank you! Yes, I think that would be for the best!"

When life gives you lemons, make lemonade! With a new perspective on a tough situation, I could change it into an opportunity!

∽ Chapter 7 Episode 3 ∽
Carme's Concerns, Part 1

~Carme Norad's Story~

I was awakened by a pleasant aroma—breakfast prepared by Chelma… But there was a brand new scent in the air this morning. It was pleasant, but I was eager to know what it was. This calming morning routine had been going on for over half a year, and I had grown accustomed to it.

With a few guesses as to the morning's menu, I got dressed and headed down to the dining room of the dormitory.

"Oh, good morning!"

For some reason, my boss was helping prepare breakfast.

"Good morning," I answered. "You've made it early today." He also managed the north mines, so he usually commuted from there; he was seldom around here this early in the morning. I asked him what had happened.

"I stopped by Serge's shop before going home, and we got carried away. We went straight to the Merchant's Guild to see the guildmaster where *he* got carried away… Before I knew it, it had gotten quite late. The guildmaster was kind enough to let me sleep in the breakroom of the guild."

"That explains it…" So he'd never gone home in the first place. If he rested well with that sleeping arrangement, it wasn't my place to question it, but there was one thing I was curious about.

"What did you talk about with Master Serge and the guildmaster?"

"Well, it shouldn't affect the business at the laundry shop, but I wanted to let everyone know that—"

"Good morning!"

Jane and the others had arrived.

"Chief?!"

"There he is, in the flesh."

"Good morning, sir."

"Good morning. Oh, Carme, I'll tell you the specifics after breakfast."

"Yes, sir."

He went back to the kitchen to help prepare breakfast. He had been out late last night discussing whatever it was he was discussing, and now he was helping out in the kitchen from the crack of dawn... I wondered if he was getting enough rest.

In the meantime, the other employees poured into the dining hall. Soon breakfast was served, and our boss told us that ridiculous story like it was an everyday occurrence.

"So you're diversifying into other industries?"

"To me, it's a bit of preparation for my return to the Sea of Trees of Syrus and an investment in myself so I can accumulate more knowledge and better techniques. To that end, I suppose I will be diversifying."

I understood what he was saying about preparations. While he could use space magic, which allowed him to carry much more cargo than others and have a safe space to sleep at night, I had heard that adventurers were often put into situations where the only resource they could rely on was themselves. And here he was, about to venture into a place that would make the top five list of most dangerous places in the nation. It was entirely plausible that he'd find himself in a situation where he would want to stock up on magical energy or would find himself unable to cast magic at all. If such a situation were to arise, he needed a different solution than magic. Of course, he would want to set up as high-quality camping gear and food as he could get to ensure that he could rest his mind and body well under those circumstances.

Even I remembered how I camped along the way to Gimul and ate preserved food that didn't taste good by any stretch of the imagination; I was exhausted after I arrived. I had learned the hard way that traveling, even for a non-adventurer under the protection of guard, could wear you down fast. It only seemed natural that an adventurer who regularly traveled and camped, and who had money to spend, would want to pack the best quality goods.

But in what world does an adventurer jump to the solution of developing preserved food on his own...? Only in this one, I suppose. What's more, he apparently has many more ideas that he wants to accomplish. Evidently, his long conversation last night involved discussion of how much he was going to diversify, and how much contact, groundwork, and money would be required to do so. Plus, he had written letters for the guildmasters of the other guilds and the duke, landing him a spot on the guildmasters' conference scheduled for three days from now...

"Hey, how much of that was real?" Hudom, the new hire, asked me. "I'm having a hard time believing all of that."

"It's all as real as my hand in front of my eyes."

In fact, the rest of the staff were surprised but understanding; this wasn't our first rodeo. Of course, the 'normal' reaction belonged to Hudom.

Starting with the boss' itinerary from last night, a guildmaster tended not to accommodate last-minute visitors, let alone talk late into the night, with how busy they usually were. For such a well-known merchant as Master Serge, it was plausible that the guild would accommodate him, especially for urgent matters, but any guild would have had one of their men take a message and pass it along to the guildmaster at a later date. He was treated better than anyone could have expected, but one explanation made sense, considering the array of issues plaguing the city with the influx of workers.

"Job creation..." I muttered.

"You too, Carme...? Serge and Glissela said the same thing. I've been telling everyone that isn't something I can just do on my own. I'm just investing in my future. I won't deny that there'll be a few extra jobs to go around at the end of the day."

I couldn't quite believe that he would do all of that solely for his own benefit. He always claimed that the laundry shop was a sort of insurance policy—that is, a source of steady income. *Still, all he ever worries about is how the employees and slimes are treated, as well as our working conditions. Granted, that does net him satisfied employees, myself included, and high morale... But customers are next in line, and he always puts himself on the back burner.*

This was something I was told to keep in mind when I was first sent to this shop by Master Serge, but I still would have been concerned about it without him having to tell me. Our boss just liked people a little too much. It was a virtue, certainly, but a precarious one for a businessman. I had a feeling that his selfless nature was what my sister and I were sent here to help him out with.

"Well, you definitely have a lot of preparations to make."

"Exactly. I'd want to be prepared heading into a dangerous area like that."

While true, it sounded like an excuse to create those jobs, to me. As far as I could see, the other employees seemed to share my sentiment. No one would say anything, but no one was buying our boss's excuse either. As for Hudom, he was still doubting whether his new boss was being serious… I couldn't blame him.

Of course, he does seem to have more than enough capital for the new business. If it was too risky of a venture, Master Serge or one of the guildmasters would have stopped him. If they're willing to move forward with this, the endeavor was worth it. All I can do is continue to run the shop as best I can, and maybe eventually…

"Oh, speaking of… You asked me to look into other laundry shops that have appeared."

"I did, right before I left for Fatoma. Did you find out anything?"

"More than nine in ten of the shops have folded. Without any cleaner slimes, and the need to rely on manpower to perform the laundry, I don't think they were able to compete with us in terms of speed, quality, or price…but surprisingly, there is one shop that is still in business."

"Really? What sort of shop is it?"

"A shop in the west end, run by a mother of two young children out of her home and former workshop."

"How is their business doing?"

"Terribly. They seemed to be just getting by with the support of their friends and neighbors; her husband, who passed away last year, was very well respected."

"I see… We're on the east end, so having a branch in the west would make it more convenient for customers over there. I remember we do have many clients from the west since the refinery and a lot of workshops are over that way. It's a good location, and it would be great to have someone already established in the community to help us start up. Of course, she may have her own thoughts on the matter; we can't leave her out of the discussion. We should present our intentions for a buyout to her and explain the structure of management if she accepts."

"That sounds reasonable. That would be a task too daunting for me, and some people may consider it a lack of respect if the actual owner is absent in the negotiations. I will help prepare for it, of course, and can accompany you to assist in the details of the contact."

"Absolutely. Could you run me through the process of a buyout and the etiquette surrounding them? It's all new to me."

"Certainly, sir. Let us finish our breakfast first."

After breakfast, we promptly moved to the office of the shop. We spent the day running through the process of a buyout, creating the necessary documents and contacting the business in the west end, as well as taking care of the necessary mountains of paperwork. Were these tasks so urgent that they had to all be completed in one day? His bad habit seemed to be rearing its head again.

Speaking with Master Serge must have had some sort of influence, but my boss always surpassed my expectations. He was the kind of person to spend too much time thinking about how to make things as optimal as possible and pile onto his backlog of work.

"Chief?"

"Whoa?! Oh, Hudom… You startled me."

"Sorry, I did knock. Deep in thought, were you? Oh, did the boss go home already? Chelma asked me to bring over tea and snacks for you two."

"Yes, we finished our work for the day. He said he wanted to get back home today."

"Got it. Do you mind if I take the extra serving of these, then?"

"Go ahead. Waste not, want not."

"Thanks."

As soon as he said so, Hudom started noshing on the food. While he gave off a nonchalant attitude. I didn't find it rude.

"You guys really finished all that paperwork together?"

"Yes. What of it?"

"How's a kid his age able to do business paperwork? I couldn't have powered through even one sheet of that at his age. I could barely even sit through school."

"*That's* your concern?"

Still, it did make me curious. Where *did* he learn how to do all that paperwork? He did ask me how to fill out some parts of it, and I had gotten the impression that he wasn't used to the conventions of official paperwork when he filled some documents out for the guild, but he seemed comfortable, even skilled with the task.

"I did start learning it when I was about his age. I suppose it depends on the individual."

My workload had been quite a bit less than the average worker, but it seemed plausible that our boss, who had been through a lot, seemed capable of these things.

"I do understand that kids can be talented in different things. But as far as I can see, I don't think our boss fits that case... He's not very childlike." Hudom suddenly flashed a serious look, dramatically pausing for my input.

I couldn't help but chuckle. "You ain't wrong, that's for sure."

"Right? I mean, not that there's anything wrong with that, but something's been on my mind."

"What might that be?"

"It'd be great if I was imagining it, but hasn't he been on edge for a while?"

"How so?"

"I mean, he seemed really nervous when we first met. I was told he's a fairly chill individual, so I thought he was someone else at first. Today, it looked like he was overcompensating for his stress by forcing this cheerful demeanor..."

I was starting to understand his approach.

"What do you think?" Hudom asked.

"I didn't get the same impression as you, per se, but he seemed more focused on work today. Like he wanted to finish everything as quickly as possible, considering how busy he's going to be soon…"

"That's another thing… He went to see the president of the Morgan company, right? How did they go from him checking on the aftermath of the arson to talking about a new business venture?"

"It may take some getting used to, but his thoughts can be sporadic sometimes."

"Must be a sign of a genius. Isn't it tough talking to someone like that?"

"It can be overwhelming at times. But he's always happy to explain his thought process whenever I ask. I feel like that's a common trait among scientists… He's much better than the scientist client I knew from my old job, actually."

"I think I know the type; they rattle on about stuff no one else can understand and wonder why you're not following their logic. I guess our boss isn't that bad, relatively speaking."

That sounded quite specific…

"Do you know somebody like that, Hudom?"

He chuckled. "I've traveled all over the land looking for a challenge, so I had the chance to meet all sorts of people. Not that they aren't nice, but it can be exhausting."

We shared a laugh about that.

"Now that I think about it…" I started.

"What is it?"

"About him being on edge and not being childlike… Whenever a problem comes up, he tends to hit the ground running looking for a solution."

"What do you mean?"

"He doesn't ever get upset like a child. He handles his emotions like an adult... I dunno, it's hard to explain." I fell silent for a moment, and Hudom simply waited for me to speak again. I was beginning to see a glimpse of his seriousness in these moments.

"For example... Regarding talk of a new business at Master Serge's, it seems like a natural progression, if you consider his position as a businessman."

"Go on."

"Bluntly speaking, words of concern aren't going to put a single sute in Master Serge's pockets."

"Blunt, but true."

Of course, it must have been nice to have a friend be concerned for his safety.

"Meanwhile, there's the matter of losses he suffered from the arson—damaged merchandise and property, lost revenue during the closure, and the cost of hiring added security. There's no sense in our boss droning on about personnel and security, especially if Master Serge has already dealt with the problem at hand. That is to say, his only problem now is finances. In that sense, I think he was more grateful for a single business opportunity than a thousand words of friendship and concern."

Our boss had told us that he had inherited a great amount of money from his grandparents, and part of the new business was a slime-based factory co-sponsored by the Morgan company. Would that not include financial backing for the Morgan company on our boss's part? Master Serge wouldn't let a bit of arson kill his business, but surely it helped a lot to gain all that money when he needed it most. Even if the financial backing came in the form of a loan, our boss wouldn't try to take over the business by force.

143

As far as loans went, Master Serge could not have hoped for a better lender, and building a factory to produce more popular products would lead to more profits down the road.

"I think I get it. Kids might cry when they face a challenge, but that won't solve anything. So he jumps straight to figuring out a solution. Guess you could say he's a logical, pragmatic sort of person."

It sounded like Hudom was catching on.

"He can be a bit strange when he's always trying to bring up his slimes or talking about things he learned from who knows where. But he always tries to solve problems right away and takes the business seriously, and I find that reassuring. Ultimately, his age is irrelevant. Whatever shortcomings he may have, he makes up for them through his employees, like me."

"You really do trust him."

"I just worry that he puts too many of his eggs into one basket, so to speak."

"Now that's something I can't relate to at all. I won't do any more work than I absolutely have to... And on that note, now is one of those times, so I'll see myself out. Thanks for the chat."

"Oh, no problem."

Hudom swiftly took his cup and plate out of the office.

"At least he finished eating first."

The part about our boss being on edge was still on his mind, though. Hudom seemed more observant about people than one would assume. *I'll have to keep an eye on the boss going forward for sure.*

⮜ Chapter 7 Episode 4 ⮞
Carme's Concerns, Part 2

~Carme Norad's Story~

"Good morning!"

The next day, our boss arrived at his usual time. I noticed that he wasn't so tense, but was also a bit too cheerful, like he was trying to make up for that.

"Good morning, sir. Were you able to rest well?"

"Yes, I did go home and get some sleep. Albeit later than I intended. I noticed that more of my slimes had evolved, so…"

"Still? Please, try not to overwork yourself."

"Don't worry. I slept enough that it wouldn't affect my work, and I think the whole evolution frenzy is dying down. The slimes seemed to have stored up nutrients from the mountains of trash I was feeding them in Fatoma, so that prepared many of them to evolve. Two slimes evolved last night, and both of them evolved from sticky slimes that ate water spiders, which are commonly used for food in Fatoma. One of them is a spider slime, with skills like Nesting and Capture, and that makes me think that the water spiders were actually spiders, when I'd thought they were crabs at first… That doesn't really matter, though. The other one became a crust slime with the Molting ability. They each share their basic abilities and appearance with a sticky slime, but—"

"*AHEM*. Anyway, the laundry shop across town responded to your offer."

"They did? That's quicker than I expected."

I didn't want to cut off his little monologue, but when it came to slimes, he could talk your ear off for literally hours about them. The letter of reply from the rival laundry shop seemed to snap him out of it quite nicely. I wouldn't have minded listening to him during my lunch or after closing time, but as long as we were open for business, I needed him to get his head together; seeing the boss and his second banana standing around doing no work whatsoever would set a bad precedent to the other employees. Of course, I knew that he knew this, and he had enough common sense in him that it probably wouldn't be a major issue.

"Hm…" He pored over the letter, looking pensive. "It says we can drop by their shop anytime. I'm guessing that includes today?"

"Let me see." I took the letter from him and read it myself. His hypothesis checked out. "Seems like we can take it at face value. Unless they're busy, I wouldn't imagine they'd mind if we dropped by today."

"Wonderful. Then let's make our way there in the afternoon, after lunch. I would like us to be presentable and to avoid intruding on their lunch if we can help it."

"Yes, sir. I'll make the appropriate preparations."

That moment, perhaps because he had just mentioned being presentable, something on his arm caught my eye.

"Is that a bracelet? I've never seen you wearing one of those before."

In fact, I had never seen him wearing any jewelry whatsoever. Some people wore culturally significant accessories, regardless of age or gender, but I'd never heard him mention anything like that. And yet, clear as day, I could see a metallic strand wrapped around his left arm and looped together by a gem.

"Oh, this?" He began to chuckle, seemingly amused. "Does it look like a bracelet?"

"Isn't it a bracelet?"

"I mean, I would hope it looks close enough to one, but this is actually a slime; a wire slime that evolved in Fatoma, to be exact. It can stretch itself into thin strands. Figured I could test out combining it with a gem, so it'll look like jewelry."

"Really...?" I wondered if there was any point in substituting a slime for jewelry. Though, seeing how much he was enjoying the conversation, I decided not to bring that up.

I waited for a break in his speechifying to return his attention to the shop.

■ ■ ■

After lunch, the boss and I had gotten ourselves in order, and we found Hudom ready to accompany us on bodyguard duty.

"Thanks for coming along, Hudom."

"No problem!"

Hearing that our boss had personally asked him to guard us, I was secretly surprised; he hardly ever had guards accompany him.

I knew by this point that he was an adventurer, and a very capable one at that, but I mostly saw him as an unusually precocious child when we first met. Once the shop began to do well and we started facing disruptions, I recommended that he hire dedicated guards numerous times. While he usually was very receptive to suggestions from me and my sister, he would always refuse any security in a gentle but firm manner, reassuring us that he was an adventurer who could handle himself. The only exception was when I asked Fey to accompany him, as a formality, to the Duke's residence.

He had recruited quite a powerful team—Fey, Lilyn, Dolce, and Ox. When it came to guarding our little shop, this group was practically overkill. But he had zero interest in hiring guards for himself. Of course, your average bodyguard may be less of a protective force and more of a hindrance.

"Is something wrong, Carme? I feel like you're staring at me."

Now that he mentioned it, I guess I was. "I just never expected you to ask for a bodyguard."

"What…? Right. You and Carla have always been pestering me about that."

He seemed to remember how he had turned down those suggestions too. He looked away, feeling awkward.

"I'm not upset. I understand how capable you are, sir. I'm just genuinely curious as to why you decided to invite Hudom."

"I hear the city's becoming more dangerous. I saw people getting arrested just this morning. Besides, my suit is a bit restricting when it comes to movement. Oh, but maybe I could use a moveable suit made from monster hide or something."

"Formal wear you can move around in?" Hudom chimed in. "I don't know if it will suffice in combat, but it might have demand on its own. No harm in being more comfortable."

Come to think of it, on his commute from the northern mines, he would pass the north gate, where the penitentiary was. That explained why he saw people getting arrested, but this was not his first time there… Was it just for added safety because of his outfit?

"Even just the joints…" Their discussion continued.

"I was at this place one time, and…"

"With that sort of hide and plants?! There are so many different monsters out there. I suppose you could…"

But this wasn't the time for a lengthy discussion on designing breathable formal wear.

"Sir, I admire your creativity in generating new ideas from everyday conversations, but you're being a little too enthusiastic right now."

"Oh, sorry. We'll pick this up later, Hudom."

"Yessir!"

He certainly had a one-track mind... As a man of business, I couldn't let them openly discuss a potentially huge venture in the middle of the street. On a few occasions, I had considered Master Serge and the guildmaster to be overprotective, but seeing him act like this must have been concerning.

I followed the pair as they shifted to discussing various things about the scenery we were passing.

■ ■ ■

"Um... Carme?"

"Yes?"

"That's the laundry shop, right?"

"Pretty sure..."

We were halted halfway down the street the laundry shop stood on. There was a swarm of people a few steps from the establishment, comprised of well-built young men holding hammers and pieces of lumber. They didn't look like patrons, and there was palpable tension in the air.

"Might've come at a bad time, Chief. What now?" asked Hudom.

"Some of them have already noticed us... Even if we reschedule, we need to ask what works for them first. If things get dicey, you know what to do," he added, his tone having gotten more serious, and dauntlessly approached the crowd. Hudom and I stayed close to him on either side. As we grew closer, many investigative looks came from the crowd.

"Excuse me." Once we were about a horse's length away from them, the boss spoke up. "If you don't mind me asking, what happened here?"

The crowd muttered for a few seconds before one of them answered, "Nothing."

It sure didn't seem like nothing.

"I see. Could you let us through, please? We have business with the shop over there," our boss answered.

The man's expression rapidly switched from one of indignation to rage. "Business? What kind of business?"

"Um, are you a representative of the shop?"

"None of your damn business!"

"It is, actually," I interjected. The man shot a nasty look at me; nothing I didn't expect, though. "We're here to negotiate with the owner of this shop. We have no obligation to disclose the nature of our meeting; after all, this concerns our own reputation as a business. Obviously, we'd want to be sure of who we're speaking with, yes? The owner has already been informed via mail. If you are not representing the shop, I'll have to ask you to move aside." That seemed to quash any retort he might have been concocting.

After a few seconds, he snarled, "All that crap about... I knew it! So *you're* the one trying to steal this shop with some phony contract!"

"Huh?" What was he on about?

"Surprised you brought this little punk along. Guess that explains why he ain't afraid."

"No, our boss simply—"

"Enough talk! We know all about that letter! You intended to buy out that shop, in writing!"

"But—"

We had indeed sent a letter introducing the idea of a buyout, but they had gotten the wrong impression entirely. I could recall the contents of the letter. Our objective was to provide greater convenience for customers and to separate the clientele into multiple locations in order to lighten the load on the shop. Our offer was to buy out their workshop and homestead, or the workshop alone; this was, of course, open to negotiation. In the event of a buyout, any employees who wished would be permitted to continue their employment, and no one would be asked to vacate the premises. The main difference would be the change in workdays; we would have them follow the main of Bamboo Forest. That being said, we would try our best to not disrupt any existing employee structure.

That was the gist of it, I was sure. We had no intention of kicking out the family. In fact, we would even prefer that they kept working here, so I didn't think it was fair for us to be met with this kind of response.

"Hold on a minute," I spoke up. "Let's have a calm, collected discus—"

"Bullshit! We know exactly what you people do—you fleece others into giving you their hard-earned money, or even their homes!"

"Damn straight!"

"You know how many of us got no roof over our heads thanks to *you*?!"

"You think we wouldn't remember that shady-looking guy trying to force them into selling the place?!" The others started joining in.

So from the sound of things, there's already been a few evictions, and someone's already been here trying to put the screws on the owner to sell the workshop...

"Carme."

"Yes, sir. I have the same feeling as you."

"This is definitely a case of mistaken identity."

We had been hearing about the problems plaguing the city, and this part of town was no exception. I believed these men when they said someone was out there duping people into selling their homes. But that wasn't us.

"I think I understand what you are talking about. We are not affiliated with those people. We run a laundry shop on the east end, Bamboo Forest."

I followed my boss's lead. "The owner of this laundry shop has extended an invitation to us to stop by any time."

"Bamboo Forest? I know that place."

"Our workshop uses them."

"She answered their letter?"

"Rumor has it, a kid manages the place... Is that the kid?"

It sounded like some of them knew about our establishment.

Just as the crowd became more vocal, and their animosity towards us began to fade, the man who first accosted us shouted, "Don't let him sucker you! Those scammers like to claim they're from legit businesses!"

"R-Right!"

"But I heard business is booming there."

"Yeah. Maybe if we just let him talk to—"

"Use your damn heads! How many other people got that idea and then signed a contract that screwed them over? Once you ink that contract, the guild won't lift a finger to help you! If that lady and her kids lose their home, her husband's gonna be spinning in his grave!"

With that, the expressions of those who were considering hearing us out began to darken. Maybe some of them were victims of the con artists themselves. It was a bit concerning that the guild wasn't doing anything about this, though.

"So you wanna screw our laundry shop over? I don't care how old you are! You're gonna regret you ever came here, you little shit!"

So much for the diplomatic option…

Then, our boss muttered something I couldn't hear. I turned to look at him, and he had a fire in his eyes like I'd never seen before. Sometimes I'd catch him feeling sad when reminiscing on his past, but this was different. In this moment, he seemed utterly despondent.

"What's the matter, sir?"

"I'm just disappointed. I'm sure they've been through a lot… But they're acting like a bunch of damn thugs." His voice was leaden and hopeless.

I understood where he was coming from, but…

"*Excuse me?!*"

This was hardly the right time to make that remark. Hudom moved to step between us in the crowd when the boss stopped him.

"Are you sure?" Hudom asked.

"I ran my mouth, so I'll face the consequences. Just keep Carme safe, please."

"Yes, sir…"

"You got some nerve, punk."

"The truth hurts, doesn't it?"

The situation grew all the more tense, but our boss remained defiant. "All I see here is a bunch of grown men waving weapons around, who can only shout down and intimidate anybody who gets in their way, refusing to even listen to reason. How are you any different from the thugs destroying this city?"

"Y-You little…"

I couldn't disagree, but I don't think I would have come right out and said all that directly to these people's faces. It probably wasn't doing him any favors to be this upfront with them.

"Hudom, I think I understand what you were talking about yesterday," I said.

"How so?"

"I can't quite say for sure… He usually smiles and brushes off pretty much everything. I've never seen him react like this."

I was prepared to resolve this situation by force, but then…

"You there, cowering behind the door. Might you be the owner of this shop?"

I had been too focused on the conflict at hand to notice. The door to the shop was slightly open, and a slender woman was peering through the tiny crack. She seemed to be the owner of the laundry shop.

"What the hell are you doing?! Get back inside!" the man called.

"I…"

"May I talk to you?" our boss asked.

"You shut up!"

"I just want to have a word."

"Don't worry! We'll keep you and the kids safe!"

The owner looked from us to the men, back and forth, and the man kept reassuring her.

"I'm sorry…" Finally, the owner retreated into her shop.

"Fine, then. Let's just leave," our boss declared.

In spite of the situation, he'd seemingly given up completely on his objective and turned to leave. This seemed to take the man by surprise as well. "Wha— Hey!"

"Apologies for the intrusion. I think she's made her intentions clear, so I'll be going now. I'm fairly certain you won't see us again, but if you still have complaints to voice, you can make an appointment at my shop."

"An appointment…?"

"You can make arrangements to see me directly. I assure you, I will not chicken out. You can even bring one of your little weapons along, if it makes you feel better. But if you harm or threaten any of my employees… Well, let's just say I will *deal with you appropriately.*" His voice was quiet, but extremely ominous.

"Let's get out of here, Hudom," I encouraged.

"Got it!"

The boss had already walked quite a ways ahead of us, and we soon caught up to him.

"Sir. What was all that about?"

"I'm sorry, Carme. Just forget about buying out the shop… I'm over that idea. I hate to say it, but we're better off looking for another laundry shop or building a new branch from scratch."

"If you say so. We are hardly in any hurry. Back to the drawing board, as they say."

"Yes."

After that, the conversation died, and we kept walking in silence. Our boss had a bad habit of overthinking things, and it seemed that habit had reared its ugly head in particularly egregious fashion today. I could imagine why he was so upset, but in any other situation, he would have simply brushed it off. Maybe he was stressed out enough that it was easier for this situation to get to him?

"Sir, are you sure you're all right? If I didn't know any better, I'd say that you're burning yourself out."

He opened his mouth, but nothing came out. He seemed unable to deny my accusation. After a few moments, he sighed. "Yes... I think you're right about that."

"If there's anything on your mind, I would be happy to hear you out."

"Right... Personally, I don't expect anything to come of this. But I like to err on the side of caution. That's why I have you in my shop, after all. Not to be judgmental, but if that shop's owner were to take your place, I wouldn't feel safe leaving her in charge of things."

"I completely agree. At the very least, it seemed like all that support allowed her business to stay afloat."

"True. I'm not around the shop too much, but if there's one thing I know, it's that anyone in charge of the shop, whether it's me or somebody else, has a responsibility to keep the shop and its employees safe."

Since he had realized that the lady from before couldn't do that herself, I took it to mean that he trusted me with that responsibility.

"That being said, there's no avoiding the unexpected; it usually comes without warning. No matter how careful you are, stuff can still just happen; we're only human, after all. It only takes the slightest oversight or moment of neglect to lose everything we may hold dear."

He spoke with the wisdom of a man who had lived a whole lifetime, and then chuckled. "Here I was, constantly trying to be careful, trying to mitigate as much of the unexpected as I could... but I guess that was causing me more stress than I realized."

"Maybe the state of affairs in this city played a role in that as well?"

"For sure. But ultimately, the onus is still mine. We're no different from anyone else in this city—we do what we must in order to make a living. I don't think we're cutting corners. But some people will never be content, no matter how careful you are."

"That's true."

"I need to work on that, but it's still in my nature to think about that sort of thing. So I'm afraid you're stuck with me," he said, flashing a sly grin.

"Of course. That's what I'm here for."

He smiled. "True."

We continued on our way back. The tension in the air had dissipated, and he seemed to have more of a spring in his step as he walked.

⮞ Extra Story ⮜
What Happened to the Former Manager

My lungs are howling in pain… I haven't run like this in years… Shit, every part of me hurts…!

The chilly evening air flooded my lungs, sending me into a coughing fit. My aching body was starved for oxygen, forcing me to stop and focus on steadying my breath.

"How did it all come to this…?!" I huffed, standing alone on the dark road.

I started to breathe deeply, bringing clarity to my mind, and I started to reminisce on how I'd ended up in this situation.

■ ■ ■

"Goddamn it!"

The morning after the press release, I was sprawled on the couch at home, seething with rage and anxiety.

…employee found dead in his apartment…

…known as the employer of Ryoma Takebayashi…

…sudden press conference regarding his death, after weeks of silence…

…involved in yet another scandal. The president of the company…

…internal disagreements over the wording of the press release…

I flipped through the TV channels mindlessly, and seemingly all of them were discussing the previous day's events—the press

160

release, and the assault that took place shortly before that. Baba was supposed to take the fall for everything so the media would let off the company, but that plan had gone up in smoke by now.

"Baba should've listened to the president... That stupid prick! Whenever this happens, you're *supposed* to cut off some mid-level management to placate the rubes' bloodlust! But *noooo*! Just come right out and admit everything instead, why don't you, you useless naïf?!"

I ranted frustratedly to no one but myself and sank into the couch. "Next it'll be *me* getting the sack... The hell am I supposed to do now?"

My cell phone buzzed. *A text from the boss? At this hour of the morning?*

I unlocked the screen and read over the message. "Keep your head down. Do the work you're assigned. Nothing more. Walk the line. That is all I can tell you right now."

Work? In this state of affairs?! Not like I've anything to do save for prepping Takebayashi's funeral anyway. It's all that bastard's fault anyhow... If he hadn't gone and popped his clogs, we wouldn't have to deal with any of this shit! He never shut up about his good health...

Mentally taking my grievances out on my late subordinate was very calming to me... The feeling was like that of a dose of nicotine being delivered directly into the brain of a chain smoker. Then, all of a sudden, an idea struck me.

"Wait a tick..."

I opened my briefcase and leafed through the paperwork for his funeral. "Not this, not this... Ah, found it!"

What I'd found was a stack of quotes from several different funeral homes. "Figures... Factoring in food and drinks, gratuities, and money for the priest, this is a damn hefty sum."

My mood drastically improved. With my age, finding a new line of work would be difficult, not even factoring in the ongoing barrage of bad press to my name. But the company was already as good as six feet under, just like Takebayashi. I saw little reason to leave any money on the table.

Ah, what the hell. I'll just call this a little bonus on my pension, for emotional damages. And so, I decided to skim a little from the funeral fund for myself.

That day, I met up with a friend from college at a sit-down restaurant downtown. We were clubmates back then, and I recalled how he'd gone off to work for a funeral home after graduating. Although we kept in touch for a while after that, we had gradually drifted apart. Fortunately, he still had the same phone number, and he agreed to meet me with the same friendliness as I remembered.

I gave him the run-down of my situation (minus the whole embezzlement part, obviously) and mentioned that I was looking at cost estimates for the funeral. Once he learned that I was working for the company getting cornholed on every news network, he expressed concern for my well-being and future.

There were a few articles online that went so far as to claim that I'd drunkenly assaulted Takebayashi, so I was prepared for the possibility of my friend turning me away over that. But it turned out he'd never really gotten used to this whole online thing. Hell, he was the type of person who still religiously watched the evening news on TV and strongly believed that the internet was crawling with fake news and sensationalism; he didn't trust any online news at all. Even as we wrapped up the meeting, he kept encouraging me to stay strong, and not to let all the online news outlets trying to "cancel" me get me down, since they were all just slander and lies anyway. Truth be told, he was the textbook example of a useful idiot.

"What could I do about the food and drink expenses?" I asked him. "Money's been kind of tight for me lately…"

"Well… You could go for a cheaper caterer."

"Is that an option?"

"You'll still need to feed all of the guests. That'd be the entire company in this case, so it'll still cost a fair amount. If you want the quality of a typical company-sponsored funeral, I'll have to advise you to stick with what you have."

"I get that, but I'm trying to cut corners wherever I can without botching the funeral. That scandal cost us a lot of contracts, so there's some pressure on me from up top and all."

"Mm… I see."

"Sorry to be so demanding. Also, I'd like to make this a really ostentatious affair. He always did have a thing for flashy, expensive-looking sorta crap when the company's name was involved."

"Style over substance, eh? Guy musta been a real asshole. Oh, uh, not to speak ill of the dead or anything. Just an observation."

"It's fine, no harm done."

Knowing my friend, he really meant no ill will. Not that I cared one way or the other. I certainly didn't give a damn if others looked down on Takebayashi. Actually, the thought delighted me. And the company was dead to me anyway. Even now, I was using his death as an excuse; it was almost comical.

Our meeting continued until we got to the point where my questions needed further looking into, so we parted ways for the day, with plans to pass on information to our respective companies and look into things.

In retrospect, this may have been the point where it all started to go wrong.

■ ■ ■

As soon as I returned to the office, I called over the man who was closest to Takebayashi. "Tabuchi! Get your ass over here!"

"Y-Yes, sir…! What is it?"

"You know what Takebayashi's religious beliefs were, what denomination he practiced? Need that info for the funeral."

"Oh, uh, that's fairly private info… I'm sorry, sir, I have no idea."

"You neither? Useless prick."

"Sorry…"

"Dammit, I'm running out of options… Does he have a Buddhist altar at his home, then? Should be able to figure things out that way."

"I think so… It was for his mother, if I recall."

"Good. I'm headed over to his place, then."

"T-Today?!"

"I need a pic of it for the funeral! And I need it *yesterday*!"

"Yes, sir…"

"Call the property first. Make sure they'll let us in again."

"Right, I'll call the landlord," Tabuchi said, slinking back to his desk.

If only I'd just told Tabuchi to go and take the goddamn photo himself… things wouldn't have turned out like this.

■ ■ ■

That night, I pulled into the closest parking lot to Takebayashi's apartment, with Tabuchi riding shotgun.

When we made our way to the apartment building, some grumpy-looking old fart was waiting for us. According to Tabuchi, he was the landlord. The man acted friendly to Tabuchi but gave me a real "screw you" kinda look. That really pissed me off. I almost made a comment about how if he was that upset to meet new people, he'd have trouble getting by at the retirement home, but I figured it was better that I didn't. I was dog-tired, so I decided I'd just get the photo and get the hell out.

Then, just as I made it to the room with the altar, my right pinky toe slammed into something and I cursed in pain!

"A-Are you okay, sir?!"

"Shut up and mind your own goddamn business! What kinda stupid dresser is this, anyway?!"

"That's a katana drawer. His dad was a swordsmith, and he inherited one of the pairs he'd made. One regular length, and a shorter one. He showed them to me once. The blade was so gorgeous that I almost reached out and touch—"

"Who the hell asked you?!"

"R-Right…"

"Let's just get the damn picture and go!"

I didn't want to be in this accursed place for even a second more than necessary. Just as Tabuchi was about to take the shot, the landlord appeared and offered us tea.

"Tabuchi. Go placate that old codger."

"Me? I'm trying to take the—"

"I'd like to hurry and get outta here, if you don't mind! And he clearly hates my ass anyway! Gimme that camera!"

I took the camera back from Tabuchi, and he went off to join the landlord. They started yammering on about some new snack food or some bullshit. Tabuchi called out that he'd be waiting downstairs; without responding, I got to work on taking the pictures. Mind you, this wasn't a formal photo session; it'd just take a minute. I took about a dozen photos of the altar from the front and side angles.

On my way out of the room, I once again slammed into something. This time on my left pinky toe.

"This goddamn drawer again! What a pain in the ass…"

While clutching my foot, I recalled something my friend at the funeral home told me…something about some sort of protective katana that those who followed a certain denomination would keep in their homes. Renting out replicas wasn't exactly hard to do nowadays, but evidently, those with family heirlooms would keep real ones around.

I'd considered saving on renting a katana for the funeral by taking Takebayashi's, but my logical side wasn't going to take his belongings without permission or risk being charged with theft over it. Plus, it wouldn't have been right to lay hands on a dead man's possessions.

And yet, in spite of all that, my hand reached out for the katana drawer.

If only I'd dragged my sorry ass home the moment I got those photos, there might have been hope for me yet.

Swords in general never interested me. I may have listened to Tabuchi's story with some interest, but I would have just told him to shut up anyway, that I didn't give a shit about what a dead man's family heirloom was worth. Well, there was no one around to witness me doing this anyway. Plus, having it would save me a bit of trouble.

Such were the thoughts running through my head as I slid the drawer open; it smelled of foxglove. Inside, there was a katana, housed in a simple wooden sheath. It didn't even have a sword guard on it like you'd associate with a proper Japanese katana. I sighed with relief at how unimpressive the thing looked.

Then I withdrew the katana and fell speechless. There were no words to describe how beautiful the sword was. When Tabuchi had described the pair of swords in this drawer as 'gorgeous,' I'd muttered under my breath that he was a rube with the vocabulary of a grade-schooler. But upon seeing them for myself in person, no other descriptor came to my mind—gorgeous.

The sword was almost physically drawing my eyes in, pulling me into a trance. The fact that it belonged to Takebayashi mattered less and less to me.

Everything faded away... I could have stared at that blade for hours...

Eventually, I came to and realized I was back home, with both of the swords in my hands. I was shaken. I had no recollection of how I'd gotten home, or why I had the katanas... The more I thought, though, the more I started to remember...

My own two hands had impulsively stolen both blades, along with all the certificates in the drawer. Tabuchi and the landlord were downstairs; had they noticed my thievery? The vision of me running down a deserted street to my car, and tucking the swords into the trunk, came back to me. Luckily, it seemed they hadn't noticed. After that, I had returned to Takebayashi's apartment, where he and the landlord were still engaged in small talk, and then took Tabuchi home.

"They don't even know I have them now... Before they catch on to me, I'd better hurry and—"

—*return them*. As soon as the thought entered my mind, I recoiled in revulsion and withdrew the katana from its sheath. The glimmering blade hit me like a rush of endorphins instantly. The more I stared, the less I wanted to take the blades back.

I'd better just get my head in order first. Then I'll take them back.

At the same time, I wondered how much these beautiful swords were worth. After some research, I discovered that Takebayashi's father was something of a genius. He had earned numerous awards at a remarkably young age; unsurprisingly, he'd been designated a Living National Treasure in his later years. The more I looked into it, the more exceptional praise I found, especially for his age.

Katanas made in modern times ranged from about a few thousand dollars to ten thousand dollars in price, depending on its maker. Those made by Musashi Takebayashi, however, *started* at tens of thousands of dollars during his lifetime. By now, all of his extant swords were priced at about a million dollars apiece, with a community of collectors willing to pay double or triple that.

While my first thought was to be shocked that people would pay so much for a single katana, I started to understand why as I observed the beauty of the blade in my hands. The view of its entrancing craftsmanship and the knowledge of its sky-high monetary value had wiped the option of returning the swords from my mind.

From that day on, everything in my life began to work out even better than I expected—my regular work, preparing for the funeral, covering up my embezzlement. It didn't take long for me to forget what life was like without the katanas.

A week later, the date of the funeral had arrived. I had been at the funeral parlor since early morning. While the funeral home had taken care of most of the preparations, it was my responsibility to pore through the schedules and double-check everything. Time was flying by, but I had some free time just before the ceremony; my friend had encouraged me to take a break. With a quick thanks, I headed to the room with the shorter katana.

"There you are…"

I held up the securely kept sword and drew it, its now-familiar glimmer making its presence known. Just seeing that light filled me with bliss and relaxation. Even the sheath, which I had first thought to be too simple, was growing on me. Apparently, this type of sheath was used to store a sword for decorative purposes, but the lack of color and detail brought out the pure and refined beauty of the blade.

At this point, I wanted to carry the katana around with me everywhere. I was already at the point where I wouldn't feel right if I wasn't keeping the other katana in my own car. Even leaving this short sword here seemed wrong. I kept imagining that its mystical sheen would catch someone else's eyes, prompting them to steal it from me. That's how I came into possession of them, after all…

"Huh?"

Why? Why had I let the short katana leave my hands at all? Renting a ceremonial blade could not have cost that much. I didn't want to spend a penny I didn't have to on Takebayashi, but it was too risky… What was I doing, anyway? A funeral…? What else was I…?

Questions faded from my mind as I gazed into the shimmering blade. Nothing mattered. No one had said a thing, and no one would. Everything was fine.

"Yo."

A voice made me jump. I turned to find one of the workers on my team, who had gotten the job through connections.

"K-Kurashiki? What are you doing here…?"

"Tryin' to grab a smoke. What brings you here, chief? Whoa, what's with that crazy-looking blade?"

"It's for the funeral. Just looking it over some more, since it's kind of important."

"Huh… Oh, did you know his old man was some super-famous swordsmith or something?"

"He was…?"

"No capperino on that. As for *my* old man, though, he suspended my ass, so I've been stuck in my room in front of my desktop rig all day. Took the opportunity to crawl the interwebs for all the deets about our dumpster fire of a company. There ain't nothin' about that old dickhead the media hasn't pounced on by now. You love to see it."

"I-I see…"

"So I did some research of my own, and it's like, damn, son! That guy's swords go for, like, more than I make in a month. Maybe if I'd sucked up to 'im like that fatso did, I might've gotten a sword or two of my own outta him."

"Hm…"

"I heard he had one of those swords himself. Worth a cool ten grand. Heirloom from his old man, apparently."

My heart was pounding against my ribcage. He knew how much a Musashi Takebayashi sword went for, and he even knew that Takebayashi himself had a set! What if he—

"Say, isn't that blade you got there the one he had? Don't tell me you actually s—?"

Kurashiki had a look of shock on his face. I must have been no different. Somehow, the sword in my hand had shoved itself right into Kurashiki's shoulder. His howl of pain snapped me out of my trance.

"Are—"

—*you okay?* I wanted to ask, but the words wouldn't come out. *Never mind that, he needs help, now! But if someone else saw me—*

"Ugh… What the hell?! I-Is that… No! Stay away from me, you psycho!"

"It's beautiful…"

The very katana that had just cut through a man's flesh like butter glimmered no less brilliantly than before, even with a fresh coat of blood on it. In fact, the vibrant red gave it a sinister allure. It was incredible. *So this is the true potential of this katana… This is its true sheen… I'll never let this thing go. I'll always keep it with me…*

I burst into manic laughter.

"Y-You're crazy… Somebody help me! Help!"

No, no, no! What's wrong with me?! I need to keep my mind focused on the here and now! As my mind raced, I heard several voices.

"What was that?"

"Did someone scream? That doesn't sound good…"

"We'd better see what's going on."

"Wait, didn't that sound like Kurashiki?"

Run, you asshole.

I bolted out of there.

"Whoa?!"

"Hey, isn't that the bald guy who—"

"Out of my way!"

"Augh!"

"Ugh!"

"Piss off!"

I shoved numerous people out of my way and ran to the parking lot, where I felt the eyes of the arriving guests boring into me. I heard a scream behind me, but this wasn't the time to consider who it was or where it came from.

"Shit, shit, shit… What do I do now…?!"

I leapt into my car and sped into the city without a destination. After some time, I decided to turn on the radio to calm myself.

"This is a news flash. Reports of an aggravated assault at a funeral parlor in the Tokyo area. The assailant is—"

Those assholes work fast...

I'd already made the news. In my panic, I veered onto the sidewalk and smashed into a tree. Luckily, the airbag deployed and I was unhurt. I ditched the car and ran off into the night, my precious katanas in hand...

■　■　■

And that was how I got myself wrapped up in this mess... This was all because I crossed paths with Takebayashi. He had always brought me nothing but bad fortune.

I used to be happy. I was born into a wealthy family and never wanted for anything from childhood. My grades were excellent in school and I was a decent athlete. Most importantly, I was lucky. I had many friends in college, and despite graduating into a historically stagnant job market, I didn't have much trouble getting my foot in the door.

Then, one day, a *certain* asshole took the wind right out of my sails. Takebayashi. In contrast to me, he was one unlucky son of a bitch. And just like how multiplying a positive number by a negative one gives you a negative sum, his awful luck seemed to drag me down with him. Nothing ever went my way when he was around.

My numbers at work kept falling, and I couldn't recover them no matter what I did. My friends grew distant, my subordinates began to disregard me, and my wife left me. Takebayashi was the bane of my existence and the reason I had to kiss ass to climb the ladder and step on the throats of everyone below me.

I became more and more isolated with each passing day. My best remedy for a bad mood became yelling at Takebayashi, but the way he'd take everything on the chin with that fruity little grin on his face made my skin crawl. Maybe I would've gone easier on him if he'd gotten on his knees and given me an abject, groveling apology. And now he was worm food. Son of a bitch brought me misery to his very last breath. Now I was free to return to the trouble-free days I deserved. My luck *had* been good, just how it used to be.

But now what was I? Just some asshole in evening wear covered with dirt and blood, with only a stolen set of katanas for moral support.

I'd just stabbed someone and fled the scene; the cops would be on to me by now. Numerous witnesses saw me running out of that funeral parlor; I had nowhere to run, nor hide.

"How did I fall this far…"

Just as I muttered that, there was a sudden bright light and a tremendous impact. Time slowed to a crawl. I heard the squeal of brakes. Enough info for me to discern I'd been hit by a car. Regret washed over me. I couldn't feel any pain. I understood this was the end for me.

I wish I'd never met that son of a… That was the last thought I had before everything went black.

■　■　■

A week later, I woke up to the realization that I had not died. I was strapped to a hospital bed, and someone there debriefed me on what had happened. I'd gotten some internal bruises and fractured bones; serious injuries, but nothing life-threatening. All I needed was a few weeks of rehabilitation and I'd probably be fine.

While I was unconscious, however, I'd racked up quite a few criminal charges. For a start, grand larceny for stealing Takebayashi's katanas, as well as illegal possession of a weapon. Not to mention aggravated assault and attempted murder for attacking Kurashiki and the others at the funeral parlor. On top of that, I had broken numerous traffic laws leaving the funeral home and at the scene of the accident, and finally, the cherry on top was embezzlement, since payment for the funeral had already been settled prior to the ceremony.

That day, I was denied the sweet release of death and sentenced to a living hell on earth—imprisonment.

～ Afterword ～

Hello! This is Roy, author of *By the Grace of the Gods*. I'd like to thank you for picking up this ninth volume, where the Mad Salamander arc finally comes to its conclusion. While the salamanders didn't get much screen time in hindsight, I think it's safe to say Ryoma enjoyed his time in the peaceful fishing village.

Gimul, on the other hand, has fallen from grace, with rampant crime in the streets. Shocked by the city's changes, Ryoma resolves to make a difference himself... But we start to see him act uncharacteristically.

Chasing after a dream may be fun, but it certainly isn't easy. More often than not, reality stops us somewhere along the way. Without facing reality head-on, there's no incentive to keep going, and your dream ends up being just that—a dream. How will Ryoma deal with the deteriorating city while stuck at a crossroads between dreams and reality?

Well, maybe that's reading into things too much. Feel free to appreciate the story any way you want, as the reader.

Oh, one more thing—the anime adaptation of *By the Grace of the Gods* is scheduled to start airing in October 2020! There's an official website and everything up for it, and personally, I can't wait to see it.

Once again, thank you for your continued support of this series.

By the Grace of the Gods

10

Roy
Illust. Ririnra

VOLUME 10
ON SALE
OCTOBER 2022!